Linda,

Climb Strong,

Climbing Companions

Lori Ramirez

LORI SALIERNO

Climbing Companions

Arriving at a quiet place, Jesus sat down and taught his climbing companions.

Celebrate Life International, Inc.

To Rena Marvel Hess and Martha Maldonado de Araujo
my two mothers and encouragers in life.
You have modeled consistently over the entirety of your life
the way of Jesus and what it means to take
the high road at every turn.
Thank you for showing me the way of the Master.

Kids may not be everyone's passion, but they are everyone's responsibility.

Contents

Acknowledgement

So much goes into writing a book and there are many people who make it possible. I want to thank some very special people who made Climbing Companions a reality through their ministry efforts and prayers.

I want to start by thanking Brian Matas a million times over. Thank you for your commitment and tireless effort to make sure this book's content was accurate and grammatically correct. You are an amazing editor. Your skillful competence and meticulous attention to details were much appreciated. Thank you for your life-long friendship.

Alyssa Peterson-DeWitt, I can say without a doubt that you are one of the most incredible and amazing assistants I have ever had in my life. You are gentle but fierce, intelligent but humble, strong but kind, compassionate but a risk taker. You juggled many tasks and responsibilities to make this book possible. It is a great honor to have you as a ministry partner.

I am humbled and beyond grateful for the fun, competent and motivating men and women that lead our nonprofit chapters across the USA and around the world. Thank you, Richard Doe, Walter Allen, Jacob Mack, Teresa Lutz, Tim Tippins, Michelle Sosa, and Dominique Adonis. Your countless hours of recruiting mentors and mentoring kids make you my heroes.

I want to thank our persistent, hilarious and always-going-above-and-beyond team at the Global Support Center. In particular, Felisha Hunter, Michele Robbins, Jeanette Goodlow, Kathy Parker, Ronda Taylor, Shakirat Ayodeji, Kianna Harrison, and Wyatt Richardson for the sacrificial way you serve daily. You are my heart.

I am also extremely thankful for our phenomenal chapter support teams. Thank you, Tamara Kerr, Jason Morgan, Rachel Adams-Kelly, Mariah Getsch, and Leslieanne Doe, for the effort you exert daily to make sure kids will be reached with the truth. You are true leaders who serve. I love you.

I am grateful to Craig Riley who consistently encouraged me to get this material in print for the purpose of reaching a generation for Christ. Thank you for your belief in me and for your constant patience.

And to my good friends, Lane and Laura Smothers, I thank you. You were incredibly generous to let us escape to your gorgeous mountain cabin where much of the writing was done.

Finally, and most significantly, I want to thank my soul mate, best friend, husband, and co-writer of Climbing Companions, José Maldonado. The endless discussions, hours of writing and constant sharing of ideas have made Climbing Companions possible. No other individual has influenced me more in what it means to follow Christ than you. I love every minute of being married to you.

1

The Invitation

"It is the same with my word. I send it out, and it always produces fruit. It will accomplish all I want it to, and it will prosper everywhere I send it."[1]

A couple of years ago I was struck by the realization that 100% of the words of truth that come out of a godly person's mouth will have an effect on those who hear them. Not half, not 75%, or even 99.99% but 100% of those words will achieve the purpose for which they were spoken. I am talking about words given to a person by the Creator of the universe so they can speak them out.

Some people may be skeptical while others may have already come to the same realization of what I shared above. I share this with you because it is that realization that became a strong motivating force behind me writing this book.

I hope that what I share in this book can be of help in your quest to gain additional spiritual maturity while encouraging you to pass truth to the next generation.

I am reminded of a funny yet insightful story I heard several years ago. A family had a priceless heirloom that had been passed down through several generations; it was a beautiful vase. One day, the parents left the teenagers at home while they went out shopping. Several hours later the parents returned home to find their children waiting for them at the front door. With a sad face and a downcast spirit, the elder teen said, "Mom, Dad ... You know that beautiful and priceless heirloom that has been passed down through multiple generations within our family? Well, our generation just dropped it."

This story presents us with a great illustration. Have you stopped and wondered what happens when a generation does not pass down the baton of God's truth to the next generation? I am afraid that it would be just like the priceless heirloom in the story, it would break, and it would be there no more. I eagerly hope that this book will encourage you to pursue your own spiritual maturity with much passion so you can then pass the priceless heirloom of God's truth to the next generation. As you know, we cannot pass on to our children that which we do not possess.

God has chosen to use us as his mouthpiece.[2] We need to accept the call to be truth bearers. Throughout this book, I want to encourage you to receive the responsibility of showing the younger generation that there is a great and positive way to live their lives. I will also urge you to share God's truth.

Allow me to get back to what I mentioned in the first paragraph when I said that 100% of the words of truth from a godly person will have an impact on those who hear them. It is impossible for that not to be true. Whether it transforms the lives of those who hear or not is up to the individual because transformation is a personal choice. But the words of the prophets recorded in the Christian scriptures serve to remind us that God has promised that his truth will achieve the purpose he desires: "so is my word that goes out from my mouth: It will not return to me empty, but will accomplish what I desire and achieve the purpose for which I sent it."[3]

The way that promise of God works is a mystery to me. However, I have learned that I don't have to understand all the intricate details of how his promises work in the spiritual world because I have often enough seen their end result in countless numbers of lives in the physical world. The Jewish prophet Isaiah was inspired to remind us that God's ways are not the same as our human ways: " 'For my thoughts are not your thoughts, neither are your ways my ways,' declares the Lord."[4]

I hope this realization of what happens when God's truth is spoken to others will be a great encouragement for you as it is for me when we teach and instruct others. When it appears that nothing is happening or that people are not listening, we can still know that whoever hears God's truth will be influenced and impacted.[5]

Should we choose not to take the responsibility of passing down the baton of truth, we will end up with a generation completely removed from God's purposes and ways. It may not be everyone's passion to work with kids, but it is everyone's responsibility. Each generation has been given the ominous task of passing God's truth down to the next generation. Depending on how well we do that will determine the future spiritual condition of our nation and world.

This book is divided into chapters that follow the teachings of Jesus the Nazarene to the crowds who one day long ago followed him up a mountain to listen to his teachings and learn more from him.[6] At the end of each chapter, I provided you with a *Take Away* nugget that serves as the bottom line for the chapter. I have also provided you with a nugget that you can share with someone else. I call this nugget a *Give Away*.

Let this book be an invitation for you to either become or continue to be a *climbing companion* of Jesus. His climbing companions are the kind of people who are willing to change and surrender their lives to a new and revolutionary way of life. It is a superior way to live. It is what I call the way of the Master. Let's mountain climb together!

* * *

2

Universal Principles

"When Jesus saw his ministry drawing huge crowds, he climbed a hillside. Those who were apprenticed to him, the committed, climbed with him. Arriving at a quiet place, he sat down and taught his climbing companions."[1]

It was a beautiful and sunny day in the Pacific Northwest when I came home early from school. My dad asked me why I was home so early. I am not quite sure why this came to my mind, but I answered him by saying, "I told Ms. Smith to *shut-up* and she sent me home."

My dad's eyes grew big and I could see he was having a hard time grasping what I had just said. He tried to find the right words to question me and finally said, "How can that be?"

I replied, "No big deal. I told her to *shut up* and she said I had to go home."

My dad was shocked. I was silently enjoying his reaction. I could see him trying to come to grips with what I was saying.

Then, he looked straight into my eyes and said, "Get in the car. We are going to school to see Ms. Smith."

I immediately replied, "No dad! I am not going back to school!"
He insisted, "Get in the car. We are going now!"

"Dad, I was just playing a joke on you. I came home early because it's early release for the whole school. Honest!"

"Get in the car! We are going and talking with Ms. Smith today!"

I had no choice but to get in the car. All the while, I was thinking, "Why did I play this prank on my dad? I could have just enjoyed being home early from school."

We arrived at my school, and my dad ordered me to take him to Ms. Smith's classroom. When we got there, we found her working at her desk. My dad immediately walked up to her and after saying a quick hello asked her why I was sent home early from school. She explained that it was early release and that all students were sent home early. My dad went on to explain to her what I had told him at home. Ms. Smith was shocked. She told him that nothing like that had taken place.

My dad then asked Ms. Smith, "How is Lori doing in your class and in school?"

Ms. Smith replied, "Well, she is a good student, but she has a mouth on her. I ask her to be quiet and concentrate on her work and she usually starts talking and disturbing her friends some 30 seconds after that. She could do even better in my class if she could just stop talking."

My dad thanked Ms. Smith for speaking with him, and we went back home. All during our drive home, I knew I was in trouble. My dad was a stickler for what he called living a principled life.

When we got home, I wanted to run into my room and be done with the whole charade. However, my dad had other plans. He sat me down and began what I knew would be a very long teachable moment.

He went on to explain how honesty is a principle by which everyone must live. The lesson went on and on. The consequences came after that. I can't even remember all the things I had to do to make up for what I did, but they were many.

When I think back to that day, I cringe. Unfortunately, that was not the only teachable moment I had throughout my childhood and teenage years. When I look back on those years, it felt like I was climbing a mountain. I'd conquer one peak and take a deep breath just in time to be ready for the next one. My mom and dad never gave up teaching my brothers and me about living a principled life. My dad is in heaven now, and I hope he can hear me when I say, "Thank you for not giving up, dad." My mother is alive and well, and I often thank her for staying the course to guide my brothers and me.

Author Eugene H. Peterson uses an interesting name for those men, women, and children who were following Jesus at the time when he preached what most people today know as the Sermon on the Mount. In his Bible version, The Message, Peterson refers to them as Jesus' *climbing companions.*[2]

On that day, Jesus chose to climb up a mountain and waited to see who would follow him from the crowd that had gathered at the bottom. It makes me think that he wanted to see who was really committed to learning how to live a godly life.

In this book, I want to encourage you to either become one or continue to be a *climbing companion* of Jesus. His climbing companions are those who are willing to change and surrender their lives to a new and revolutionary way of life. It is a superior way to live. It is what I call *the way of the Master.*

As Jesus taught his climbing companions on the side of that mountain, he shared with them what many of us know today as The Beatitudes. He taught them a set of principles that explain that God's kingdom is offered to those who will learn this superior way to live and offer themselves in full surrender to that truth.

Why is this way of life considered superior? It is superior because it describes a life that is founded on universal truths. Truths by which we can live and that are true for anyone, anywhere, and anytime. These transformational truths govern the heavens and the earth and everything in between; they govern the universe. Jesus used the word *blessed* when he spoke of those living by each of these truths. Blessed is more than *happiness*, it is the highest *well-being* by which we were created to live. The Beatitudes are universal principles that bring Purpose, Power, and Peace to you and me:

- Purpose: When one becomes a climbing companion of Jesus, these universal principles show us why we were born and highlight the reason for our existence. We start seeing why God created us. A climbing companion is confident in who they are and whose they are.
- Power: The life of a climbing companion is one of empowerment. We are empowered to overcome anything that is thrown at us. Whether that is harsh circumstances, difficult relationships, or devastating emotions. These universal principles empower us to take the moral high road at every turn. Nothing can ruin our lives because universal principles give us a divine perspective along with the power to face our difficulties.
- Peace: The life of a climbing companion is also one of peace. Climbing companions have the anchored faith that God is in control of all the aspects of their life. They trust that ultimately everything is going to be alright even while facing

great challenges in their lives. Climbing companions also make the decision to honor God in every situation.

But what good is it for us to learn these universal principles and then hide them under the bed?[3] I hope the words in this book will not only encourage you to live a principled life but also encourage you to model and teach these universal principles to the kids in your home, your schools, and your neighborhood.

You may not see yourself as a teacher or a mentor, but I think we all need to fulfill that role. Some of us may say, "Wait a minute, I don't have time for mentoring," or "I already raised my own kids." That may be true, but the thing is, we, really do not have a choice in this matter. No choice at all! The *learning* followed by the *teaching* of these universal principles is a mandate that has already been given to all climbing companions of Jesus. It goes like this: "Write these commandments that I've given you today on your hearts. Get them inside of you and then get them inside your children."[4]

As you and I continue to grow and live the life of a climbing companion, we are constantly reminded that going deep is the way of the Master. Slowly but surely, we feel compelled to multiply our legacy by teaching and sharing these universal principles with others. Besides, why wouldn't we want to share them with children all around us since we naturally want the best for them?

When we choose to live our life by universal principles, we receive the benefit of that choice. When we don't, we end up breaking ourselves up against them and dealing with the consequences. That is why we want to share these truths with others, especially, our up-and-coming generation. The Beatitudes bring conviction of wrong and compel us to want to do what is right. They provide shelter and protection to those who choose to live by them.

Keep in mind that when we share these universal principles with someone, we may or may not see immediate results or see the full benefit of what God is doing in that person's life. Our job is to continue making those deposits.

I have had the privilege of speaking with mentors all around our beautiful country and have heard great stories about the transformed lives of many children and youth who are under their mentoring. Another comment that I often hear is, "I'm learning and growing just as much, or even more, than the young people I am mentoring with these universal principles." I think that is exciting, isn't it?

On the other hand, I have also heard from mentors who tell me they are struggling. They tell me things like, "I don't think I'm making much of a difference with these kids!"

If you find yourself discouraged when you parent, teach, or mentor young people, remember that as climbing companions of Jesus, our job is mainly to share and deposit the seeds of truth into their lives. We can do our best, but we can never guarantee that those seeds will germinate into a great harvest. We also need to keep in mind that some other person in a distant future may be the one who ends up reaping the fruit of the deposits that we make in someone's life.

One of Jesus' early climbing companions reminded us of something that Jesus himself told those who were following him. Jesus said, "Others have done the hard work, and you have reaped the benefits of their labor."[5] Many times, we are the *others* that Jesus talked about. We do the hard work of planting the seeds in order that someone else in the future can fully share the Good News and reap the benefit of our labor. Being the *others* is not a glamorous title or a coveted job description but that is the way it works when you climb with him. It may not be the way we want it to be but that is the way of the Master.

Something else that I often hear from people whom I meet as I travel is that sharing truth without sharing the name of Jesus does not work. As you probably know, those who mentor kids in public schools are required to stay away from religious teachings. Consequently, asking a child to dedicate his or her life to follow Jesus is not a conversation that can take place in a public school classroom. So, some people give up and walk away from the opportunity to teach godly universal truths in our public schools because cannot have it their way.

I think sometimes we forget that we are not the ones who save people; Jesus Christ is the *only* one who saves. It is the Holy Spirit the one who prompts and creates in someone the desire to come clean and purify their hearts, mind, and soul. We are merely his instrument, his messenger, and his mouthpiece to speak his truth. All the while, God through his almighty power is working on those who hear that truth. It would be presumptuous of me to think that I am the one who can get kids spiritually right with God. I *must* simply lift up his truth and trust that he will do the rest.

Something that gives me great excitement about the work of mentoring young people in our world today is that we are like the people of Israel in the Older Testament of the Bible. They were fighting battles for God on a regular basis. They did their share of the fighting until they could do no more. Then, God came and delivered victory to them. Our battles look different, but we are his warriors today—prince and princess warriors fighting against evil. We get to fight for him! It just doesn't get any better than that! Come on, are you still with me? Can you share in the excitement with me?

Let us say that we get up in the morning and we know that today is the day we are going to a public school to mentor some kids. We warm up and stretch a bit, and then we put on the full armor God has given us.[6] Once we are fully dressed, we stretch a bit more and walk out the door. We arrive and park our car in the school's parking lot. We walk into the school with our chins up high. We are ready for battle.

I don't know what weapons you prefer, for I am partial to the sword, but you may be more skilled with the shield to deflect the flaming arrows. Whatever your weapon of choice is, offensive or defensive, we get to be right in the middle of the battle. We get to share the very same universal truths that Jesus taught to his climbing companions more than two thousand years ago. I tremble thinking of it. We do our part in that classroom and then we know the Lord will do the rest. Once the school bell rings, the battle is over, and we live to fight another day. Then one day, when we least expect it or even know it, *others* will reap the benefit of our labor. Those kids for whom we fought will be ushered into the Kingdom of Heaven because you and I were willing to share Jesus' universal principles with them. We showed them the way of the Master.

Please know that at times, the life of a climbing companion seems to be an impossible one. I know that fully living out the Beatitudes cannot be done without God's Spirit giving us the strength to persevere. It also requires that we admit that we need forgiveness for our wrongs and clearly ask for that forgiveness. It takes work and blessings from above, but we can do it if we stay the course.

The life of a climbing companion requires a willingness to live a continual life of surrender and obedience to the Master. It may not be easy, but I assure that it is worth the effort. We learn and do what we need to do to get right with God so that we can then confidently share these universal truths with kids (and adults) who cross our path. We also go forward with the confidence that sooner or later they will get to the point of conviction and ask the Lord for the forgiveness of their wrongs.

I had a conversation with a woman who told me that she had decided to walk away from her Christian faith. I asked her why she would do such a thing. She said that following Jesus was impossible and that she could not do it anymore. This was my response to her, "You are right, it is impossible! No human being can live that life based on her or his own efforts."

If we find ourselves in a situation like that, admitting that we give up is the beginning of living the life of a climbing companion of Jesus. We must surrender and obey. This kind of surrender is not a bad thing, it is just admitting that we need divine help. When we do this, the Lord can begin to help us. Otherwise, the way of the Master is *impossible*. Jesus was clear about this when he asked us to be *poor in spirit* and be ready to *mourn.*[7] In other words, God will begin helping us when we put aside our spiritual arrogance and mourn over our sins in repentance.

I wanted that woman to understand that we do not live *for* Christ, but instead, we must live *by* Christ. That means that we don't just follow a set of rules, but we make every effort to live our lives following his words and teachings all the while asking him to help us do it. In other words, Jesus Christ in us, through us, and for us. That is the life of a climbing companion. As we live by these remarkable truths, we will experience a depth that can come in no other way. We make the commitment and then he helps us with it. That is the way of the Master.

So, the big question is **why should we teach these universal**

13

principles to people who are far from God if it is the impossible life? How can a grandchild, a student in the public schools, or an adult in our office live by these universal principles if these folks don't know anything about Jesus and his teachings? They don't even know how to ask God's Spirit to help them?

First of all, we know that these universal principles provide protection to those who choose to live by them. When we live a principled-based life, we fall under God's umbrella of protection. For we know that, "The righteous person may have many troubles, but the LORD delivers him from them all."[8] That by itself is a great reason why we should want kids (and adults) to learn what it means to be righteous and follow these principles. Who wouldn't want to be protected like that?

But a much bigger reason for teaching God's universal principles is that we know that when those truths are taught within the context of a positive mentoring relationship with a spirit of celebration, those principles develop in young people a desire for *wanting* to live the superior life. And sooner rather than later, they also develop a hunger to know more about the Creator of those universal truths. Wouldn't you want to be the one who plants the seeds that God can use to make this happen?

I am sure you have heard this quoted to you or someone else, "To whom much is given, from that person much is expected."[9] I know my parents gave much to me through many years of teaching and putting up with me. Knowing that places a great sense of responsibility on my shoulders. I must make every effort to give back; I cannot think of a better way than to teach young people all the positive things that were taught to me. Has anyone throughout your life invested in you? I am sure the answer is *yes*. Honor them by passing it on and helping others. That is why I invite you to join me in being the *others* and planting seeds to help our next generation learn these universal truths.

The time is now! Ready or not, here we go!

* * *

TAKE AWAY: When we establish relationships and lift his truth up, we can trust that God will handle the rest.

GIVE AWAY: Universal principles will bring purpose, power, and peace to your life.

3

Choices and Habits

"Don't become so well-adjusted to your culture that you fit into it without even thinking. Instead, fix your attention on God. You'll be changed from the inside out."[1]

I like getting up in the morning and immediately going for some type of workout. Sometimes, I choose to cycle. Sometimes, I get up and decide to walk a few miles while I memorize scriptures. Other times, I hike the mountain that is near my home. I am not overly selective as to the type of physical workout that I do each morning if I can get it done before I start my official workday. I had followed this routine most of my life until I ran into an interesting challenge.

A few days after I got married, my husband, José, told me he was going to work out with me that morning. I was delighted. As I reached for my workout clothes he said, "Let's make the bed before you go any further."

I thought a Martian was talking to me. I said, "Can you repeat that?"

He again said, "Let's make the bed."

"You can't be serious! We are getting ready to work out, not clean the house."

He calmly insisted, "Let's make the bed so we can have an orderly bedroom when we get back."

By now, I thought he was joking with me, so I laughed. But somehow, he did not think the situation was humorous. He grabbed the pillows and started fluffing them up.

I took the pillows away from his hands and asked him to look at me. He looked at me and calmly said, "We're wasting time, let's get the bed made."

I laughed and told him, "You must be joking! I've never made my bed this early in the morning. As a matter of fact, I frequently go a couple of days without making the bed."

You would have thought that I had just revealed a conspiracy to overthrow the government of the United States of America. He looked straight at me and said, "How can that be possible? Don't you know that the *habit* of making your bed in the morning sets the tone for the kind of work you will accomplish that day?"

I quickly realized this was no joke for him. He truly believed what he was saying. On the other hand, I was thinking to myself that the *habit* of working out right after you wake up is significantly more of an indicator of the kind of day that I will have.

Many mornings have come and gone since that day. I know making the bed is important to him, so I frequently help make the bed. I still enjoy my unmade bed anytime he goes on an overnight trip, but I admit that there is something good, about the habit of making the bed every morning.

There is something about the habit of doing certain good things daily in our lives. What José and I have come to agree on and believe beyond a reasonable doubt is that **habits determine our**

success or failure in life.

God gives us many great gifts and one of them is our ability to choose. The life we live has been made up of a series of daily choices. Our choices determine everything about us. The choices we make determine where we live, the level of education we achieve, the type of friends we have, the places we have visited, and much more. **Today, you and I are where our habits have brought us. Tomorrow, you and I will be where our habits will take us.**

The ability to choose is an extremely powerful tool in the hands of Jesus' climbing companions. Jesus was not only listing a series of dos and don'ts when he preached on the side of that mountain long ago, he was also explaining that we need to make choices and then make habits out of those choices. He said things to us such as be *pure in heart* and do what is *morally right*. That means we are to make those choices daily.[2]

When we decide that we want to climb in life with Jesus and obey his teachings, we are deciding that we will form certain habits in our lives. The universal principles that Jesus taught guide our choices in life and determine our habits. Author and speaker Darren Hardy said, "A choice starts a behavior; a behavior becomes a habit; a habit develops your character; your character determines your future."[3] Writer and philosopher Will Durant said, "… we are what we repeatedly do. Excellence then is not an act but a habit."[4]

Jesus' climbing companions of the past and those of today have made the choice to live by universal principles. One of those is the universal principle of integrity. As his climbing companions, we choose to be people of integrity. Because we want to please him, we make the choice to be people who are *pure-in-heart* and who work at turning that choice into a habit. It takes a series of steps to get there. We start by making the conscious choice of telling the truth whenever we speak with others and slowly but surely create that habit.

We all have that choice and can make being *pure in heart* a habit in our lives. The same can be said of the habit of respecting others even when we completely disagree with them or the habit of helping others anytime, we see a need. It all starts with the God-given ability to choose.

Imagine if we fooled ourselves into thinking that we could be pure in heart on even days and impure on odd ones, or that we could do what is morally right only one day per week. It is impossible for us to live a principled life on alternating days. There is no schedule in the world that would give us that result. Habits are those behaviors that we automatically do each day because we have done those actions repeatedly in the past.

Living a principled life develops our character, and habits are at the very heart of it. The total sum of our habits will illustrate our character. Most of us readily agree that good habits need to be ingrained within us. That ingraining process takes conscious effort. We must practice over and over until certain behaviors become habits in our lives. Trying a few times and then giving up does not build good character. It takes consistent effort and right choices.

When we are faithful to our spouse 99% of the time, we are *not* mostly faithful spouses, we are unfaithful. When we are compassionate with others 99% of the time, we are *not* mostly compassionate people, we are simply insensitive and uncaring. When we tell the truth 99% of the time, well, you have guessed it by now, we are *not* mostly honest, we are liars. **It is what we do 100% of the time that determines our moral fiber—our character.**

One of our staff members at the non-profit organization that I lead once questioned me about the concept of being people of excellence 100% of the time. I was explaining to our staff that we need to be people of excellence in all we do. I was emphasizing the habit of excellence based on Jesus' teachings about hungering and thirsting for righteousness. Jesus used some very descriptive words to encourage us, his climbing companions, to pursue those things that are excellent and praiseworthy. Our staff member said, "Are you asking us to be perfect?" I'm very glad that he asked me that question because it is important to understand the difference between being a person of strong moral fiber and someone who claims to be perfect.

I truly believe that perfection should be the goal of every climbing companion. Yes, you heard me right. But I also believe that we will only attain that perfection when we get to heaven. In the meantime, while here on earth, we ought to strive to live by God-given universal principles 100% of the time. When we fall short, we need to get back up. Those very same principles help us know when we have made a mistake and how to correct that mistake.

As an example, most of us would agree that we could lie about something sometime in our lives. Does that make us liars for the rest of their lives? Not at all. Because we, climbing companions, are people who have made a habit of telling the truth, we would quickly realize that we have lied. We would then ask for forgiveness by telling the truth and setting the record straight with those whom we offended. Then, we would go on striving to be truthful in our future dealings with others. **What I have just described is not perfection; it is rather a process called living a principled life.**

Some people who have heard me talk about choices and habits

ask me how they can go about starting a certain habit or replacing a bad habit with a good one. I don't think there is an easy answer to those questions. It all depends on our motivation and the nature of the new behavior we want to adopt. Some old habits are hard to erase, and it takes replacing them with new habits that can be strong enough to overtake the old ones.

Surgeon Maxwell Latz who authored the 1960s bestseller *Psycho-Cybernetics* reasoned that it takes a minimum of 21 days to form a habit. This was the result of his observations of the minimum amount of time it took amputees to adjust to the loss of a limb.[5] More recent studies such as those by Philippa Lally and colleagues from the University College London report that it took anywhere from 18 to 245 days with an average of 66 days for subjects of the study to turn new behaviors into automatic ones [habits].[6]

I admit that I have not done an in-depth study on this nor have somehow found the magical number of days that it takes to form a habit. But what I do know from personal experience that there is great value in doing something consistently for 21 days.

I have coached many people throughout the years who wanted to make a positive change in their life. I am talking here about significant physical, emotional, or spiritual changes in their lives. Some of my friends stopped trying after a couple of days while others stopped after a week or so. Yet, others stumbled and got back up again and again to reach the 21-day goal. Three weeks of intentionally doing something new seems to have a significant effect on most of us. Once we get there, we then have the strength to make a decision about what our next step in the process needs to be. We are better equipped to make that decision because we now have a win under our belts.

Aimlessly trying to form a new habit without a time goal is

defeating because we don't see light at the end of the tunnel. Stephen Covey's bestseller book, *The 7 Habits of Highly Effective People*, explains in detail the immense value of beginning with the end in mind.[7] We need to have a clear goal in mind. That is why having a 21-day goal as we try to make a habit is not the full answer, but it certainly is a major positive step towards accomplishing the big change that we want to make in our lives. It may be that sometimes we need to do two or three 21-day cycles before we get to our desired outcome. If the change we are after will improve the quality of our life and the power of our testimony, we ought to take these 21-day steps until we succeed.

As I mentioned earlier, I like to do a physical workout daily. It is a habit that I can now do without much thinking at all. A few years ago, I was asked to put this habit to an extreme test. I was praying about finding enough mentors and raising enough money to work with a group of at-risk kids in some public schools. I knew God would give me an answer, but I was not quite ready for the type of answer he gave me.

One night, the Lord impressed on me so strongly that I was to ride my bicycle across the United States. I really thought it was the food I had for dinner hours before rather than the Lord prompting me to do this. I went to sleep knowing this would all go away, and I could go back to praying for a safe answer the next day.

Day after day, the Lord made it clear to me that what I needed to do was to ride my bicycle across our country for the purpose of raising awareness to help those at-risk kids whom we had on a waiting list. I felt I could possibly ride 50 miles on my bicycle, but I didn't have the physical preparation required for such a long bicycle ride. I fought the idea of doing this ride across America, but the Lord would not let it go. Day after day, I prayed for another answer, but the same answer kept on coming back: ride your bicycle coast-to-coast.

Another challenge aside from the distance was finances. I knew I didn't have the money for the journey. So, I told the Lord, "Since I don't have the thousands of dollars it would take for me to pay for a good bicycle along with repair parts, a vehicle for volunteers to help me along the way, gasoline for the vehicle, food for the volunteers and me, hotel stays, I cannot go." I also told him that if the money was to *drop from the sky* I would do it, but I certainly knew that would not happen. I said, "Lord, I love you and you know that. However, I cannot pay for this ride, so I am not going. Thank you for thinking of me though."

I was happy with my decision. Even as I was driving my car the next day, I thought, "What kind of 50-plus-year-old woman jumps on a bicycle and rides across the country anyway?" It was then that I had another prompting from the Lord. It was simple, he asked me to call my dad's best friend. My dad had been in heaven for a few years and I often thought of his best friend as someone who reminded me of my dad. I had nothing to discuss with him, so I was reluctant to call him, but I decided to be obedient and call him.

His name is James. I was thinking that I was not quite sure what I would say to him when he answered my call, "Hello!"

I said, "James, this is Lori, how are you?"

He replied, "Fine Lori, what can I do for you?"

He is a busy businessman with a tight schedule, so I knew I needed to get to the point quickly, but I just didn't know what the point was. This is what happens when climbing companions answer the call of Jesus. **Sometimes, there is no time for preparation and no previously published agenda. You simply obey and go forward.**

We can easily feel like the apostle Philip when Jesus asked him to buy food for several thousand people out in the wilderness. Not only did Philip not have the money, but he also didn't know where he could go and buy such large quantities of food at that time. You probably know the story very well—Jesus ended up miraculously providing more than enough food for the many thousands of people.

So, there I was talking to my dad's best friend with a Philip-like look on my face. I am glad it was a voice-only call and not a video call with James.

James pressed me again, "Lori, what can I do for you?"

I replied, "I don't know."

My mind was going crazy, "Seriously, Lori, that is all you can come up with!"

James interrupted my thoughts, "Lori, are you missing your dad?"

"No, I am not."

"You called me. I didn't call you. You say you don't know why you called me. That's interesting. Well, I hope you have a great day, Lori."

"Well ... thanks for taking my call, James. I hope you have a great day too."

I couldn't wait to hang up the call. I was thinking about how embarrassing the whole thing was when James said, "Lori, don't hang up. I was just thinking a couple of days ago about sending your non-profit some money. Since I have you on the phone *for no reason*, will that be ok with you if I send that money?"

At that very moment, I knew what Philip must have felt like when Jesus told him to look for something to eat for all those people. The conversation must have been somewhat unreal and uncomfortable at the same time. Imagine Jesus telling Philip to go and check to see if people had something to share. (Seriously Jesus, we are talking several thousand people here.) Later, we know that Jesus told Philip and the other climbing companions that the lunch from that little boy would be sufficient.

I was having a hard time answering James, but I managed to say, "Oh, wow … yes, that would be more than ok."

I must have said goodbye to James (or at least I hope I did). James and I have had many other more *normal* conversations since then. James is one of Jesus' climbing companions and I know that he answers and obeys when the Lord calls.

After that phone call, I had no other choice but to ask Jesus to forgive my doubts and fear. I had the call from the Lord, I had the money from James, and I just needed to put my *yes* on the table. Just a few weeks later, I started my ride across the U.S. It took me 46 100-mile days to do the whole trip to raise money and awareness to help kids who were in trouble. My staff calculated that I pedaled a total of 757,000 revolutions to get from the west to the east coast of our great nation. Some people have asked me how I did it, and I simply answer, "one pedal at a time." You just need to do it over and over for 46 days.

Making small choices each hour of each day, I accomplished something that I thought I could never do. The universal principle that motivated me the most along the way was the principle of compassion. I wanted 6,000 kids to have mentors and learn about these priceless universal principles. That was strong motivation to help me pedal through the summer heat and humidity, to climb up the Rocky Mountains, the press on after a car hit me in St. Louis, to overcome sore muscles at night, and to endure sun poisoning on my hands and legs.[8]

I encourage you to think about the fact that habits determine our success or failure in life. They can also be one of the most powerful forces in our lives. The habits we develop make a difference, either positively or negatively, in our life. Without positive habits, we may not have a structure in our lives. Whatever new positive habit you are thinking about starting in your life, don't give up. Once you make the choice, set a realistic goal and go forward with confidence. Remember that it takes daily small steps and soon enough you will find yourself there.

The Christian scriptures validate the importance of habits. A habit could also be viewed as a discipline. Many have taught about spiritual disciplines that include prayer, fasting, prayer walks, keeping and honoring the Sabbath, journaling, tithing, confession, thanksgiving, memorizing scripture, and many more. Even church attendance can be considered a habit or spiritual discipline.

Marjorie J. Thompson wrote a book about various spiritual disciplines titled *Soul Feast: An Invitation to the Christian Spiritual Life.*[9] She notes that disciplines [habits] do not come naturally to us, but that "Disciplines are simply practices that train us in faithfulness. ... Such practices have consistently been experienced as vehicles of God's presence, guidance, and call in the lives of faithful seekers." Habits and disciplines enrich all areas of our life.

As Jesus' climbing companions, we know that we are called to live a principled life. As we transform ourselves and build a stronger moral fiber, we also make the commitment to show the way of the Master to others. In the 12th chapter of the book of Romans, the apostle Paul encourages us to replace the bad habit of conforming to this world with the habit of transforming ourselves by continually renewing our minds. Good established habits are the signature that every climbing companion wears. Our Christian walk is to be a lifetime of making good habits.

* * *

TAKE AWAY Good established habits are the signature that every climbing companion wears.

GIVE AWAY Our ability to choose is our most powerful life asset.

4

Respect

*"So in everything, do to others what you would have them
do to you, for this sums up the Law and the Prophets."*[1]

My dad was the senior pastor at our church during my
entire childhood and many of my adult years. Dad
always expected my brothers and me to be at church
any time the doors were open. Living next door to the church
made it easy for him and my mom to go there by themselves
earlier than anyone else. When my brothers and I were old
enough to take care of ourselves, we were instructed on how
to dress and when to be at church. Dad always expected his three
kids to sit on the front row of the sanctuary for each service.

One late afternoon, I knew I needed to get ready to go to Sunday
evening service. On that particular day, I decided that I was old
enough to show my dad that I was now the one in charge of my
life and not him. I stayed at home watching TV until I knew the
service was starting. Not bothering to change my torn jeans and
over-worn t-shirt, I made my way to the back of the sanctuary
to sit with my friend, Shanon. Once there, I made a point not to

look at my dad while he was speaking to the congregation but rather, I chose to engage in conversation with my friend.

I could *feel* my dad watching me, but I continued showing him whose authority I was now under—mine! Or so I thought! Shanon's voice sounded a bit concerned when she said, "Your dad is not happy with you."

I told her, "I know! I just need him to understand that I don't follow his rules anymore."

Shanon persisted in a loud-hush voice, "He is not happy with you and he is walking towards you!"

I thought to myself, "Surely he is not coming toward me. He would not dare interrupt his preaching. I have him where I want him."

Not more than three seconds later, I could feel his hand grabbing my arm and pulling me out of the seat.

"Lori, you will go home right now. You will change your clothes and dress properly for church. You will then walk quickly back to church and sit on the front row with your brothers. Is that clear young lady?"

I was so embarrassed when I realized that the whole church was looking at me. My well-planned disrespectful campaign had failed miserably! I stomped out of the church and went home to put on a dress. I walked back to the church with the worst attitude I could muster and went directly to the front row where my now-angelic younger brothers were quietly sitting and listening to the sermon of the senior pastor—my dad.

I knew I had failed regardless of how much disrespect I was trying to show on my face. I knew I was not in control. I knew my father was the ultimate authority in my house and he had proved it beyond a reasonable doubt. I now had the very-embarrassing job of trying to act tough in front of everyone.

When the service was over, dad asked me to stay there until he could talk to me. I thought, "Surely not another teachable moment." Soon enough everyone was gone, and dad came over to me. I tried to act tough, but my strong resolve was quickly disappearing.

Dad started, "What were you thinking, Lori Ellen? Don't you ever show such disrespect in the house of the Lord again! This is the first and last time you will do something like this. You must always show respect in the way you dress, in the way you walk, and in the way you talk."

I could not come up with anything to say to defend myself. He continued, "When I saw your disrespectful act, I had a choice to make either ignore you to avoid embarrassment in front of the church or put a stop to your act and immediately deal with you. I want you to know that I will always choose to immediately deal with disrespect from my children no matter what. Is that understood, Lori Ellen?"

I learned a very powerful lesson that day. I was trying to prove my independence, but I chose the wrong way to do it. Disrespect is never the right way to advance anyone's agenda. On that Sunday eve, I chose to violate one of the most foundational and powerful universal principles: the principle of *respect*. My father knew the importance of confronting such violation and taught me a lesson that would end up saving me from serious consequences later in life.

The non-profit organization that I lead works with some kids who are on juvenile court probation. A large percentage of them end up in juvenile court because they've violated the principle of respect. These violations come in various forms: lack of respect by physically assaulting a teacher or another student, no respect for someone else's property, not respecting curfew laws, ungovernable behavior by being disrespectful at home, and so on. When we violate the principle of respect, we quickly end up breaking ourselves up against it.

Throughout history, the principle of respect has guided countless many people to live a life worthy of honor. On the other hand, disrespect has created major havoc in our world starting thousands of years ago and continuing to our present day. In the early 60s AD, the apostle Peter wrote a letter to Jesus' climbing companions who lived in what is now the country of Turkey. Those folks were suffering persecution.

Peter urged them to keep a strong faith in Jesus and then he challenged them to live a principled life. He told them that persecution was to be expected. Peter's request to them was that they show respect to those who were accusing and persecuting them without just cause. He made it clear that choosing to live by principles would clearly show to the world that they belonged to God.[2]

I have chosen to use Peter's encouraging formula, too. The best encouragement we can ever receive is to be reminded that we belong to the Creator of the universe. When we treat others with respect, we not only validate who they are as an individual but also have an opportunity to show that we are one of Jesus' climbing companions in today's world.

You have probably read books or watched documentaries about Mahatma Gandhi and have wondered, just as I have, about how much strength it took for him to treat others with respect. He advocated peaceful resistance in the face of great adversity while pursuing human equality both in India and South Africa. His commitment to the principle of respect was admirable. Martin Luther King Jr. showed similar resolve as a leader of the civil rights movement in the United States.

Those lessons are not just good material for history books. They are very applicable lessons in our daily lives. Neither Gandhi nor MLK Jr. advocated agreement with the status quo. **Instead, they advocated treating others with respect while wholeheartedly disagreeing with them and that for which they stood.** Can you and I do that? Can we disagree with others and still treat them with respect? We certainly can!

It is impossible for us to meet someone who will agree with every single thing that we believe, say, and do. This is even true in the best marriage relationships. This is part of what makes us unique creations. It has been said, "We don't have to see eye to eye to walk arm in arm." How true!

What Gandhi, MLK, Jr., and others throughout history learned that made them so successful in their struggle was a lesson that Jesus taught his climbing companions a long time ago. This teaching was so profound that it has permeated cultures across the world for centuries. We know it as the *Golden Rule*. What an appropriate name for this powerful teaching of Jesus. It is nearly impossible to find anyone who never heard the Golden Rule quoted to them or someone else: "So in everything, do to others what you would have them do to you ..."[3]

My husband, José, and I had the privilege of visiting El Salvador a few years ago to work with some churches and speak at a handful of public schools. We also visited a juvenile prison. You heard me right, not a juvenile detention center, but a juvenile prison. Some kids as young as 10 years old were housed there. Most of the kids are older than 10 but they are kids, nevertheless. Although all our work in that country was very meaningful to us, the visit to the prison was of special significance.

Our non-profit organization had an opportunity to work with some great people in El Salvador and they had taken our materials to mentor kids in the juvenile prison. The prison is far away from the city of San Salvador and we had to travel for a couple of hours to arrive. Our Salvadoran friends, Boris and Herbert, had to jump through many hoops to make arrangements for us to visit. As the creators of the material they were using to mentor the kids in the prison, they thought it would be very meaningful for the kids to meet us.

We arrived at the prison after the long car ride and walked to the front gates. The first thing that caught our attention was the fact that all the guards had automatic weapons and balaclavas covering their faces. Herbert explained that the guards did not want the young inmates to see their faces because they, in turn, would share their identity with their gang members on the outside. If that happened, the guards' families would then be at serious risk. Talk about no respect for human life! It was sad to hear about the reason for their faces being covered.

We also learned that some folks from a church had come to the prison in the past and had been severely injured while visiting. That explained why Boris and Herbert had gone through so much trouble in order to obtain permission for us to visit. Our friends had developed a good reputation with the prison authorities because of the sacrifice they made each week so they could work with the young inmates.

I felt somewhat nervous as we walked past the security gates. Once inside, we were given quite a bit of freedom to walk around. Some of the young inmates were playing soccer with a deflated ball in a small courtyard. Others were sitting and talking.

One young man stood out. He was holding a few-months-old baby in his arms. José approached him and spoke in Spanish to him. He found out that the baby was allowed to come regularly and stay for long visits. It broke my heart to see that a baby was starting his life in such a place.

A bit later, the authorities told us that we could walk into a large room and meet with the kids who were going through our program. The room had chairs arranged in a semicircle. There was just one door and no windows. We walked through the door and were introduced to the young inmates. Our host told them that I had come from the United States to speak to them. He then motioned for me to stand in front of them. José and I stood in front of the semi-circle with our backs to the door.

I began speaking and José translated each of my sentences into Spanish for them. I spoke of universal principles and tried to encourage them to make changes in their lives. They were very receptive to my words and even smiled when I was finished.

Unbeknownst to us, some of the gang leaders were standing at the door the whole time we had been speaking to the kids. They had been *walking their signs* (speaking their silent gang language) to keep the kids inside the room from displaying much affection towards us or agreeing to what we were saying. We talked and joked with the kids a bit more after the formal presentation was over. They all kept glancing at the door and then back to us the entire time.

We said goodbye to the kids and started walking towards the door. Suddenly one of the kids looked at the gang leaders by the door, turned around and spit on me. However, we kept walking. The gang leaders did not give us much room to walk through when we got to the narrow door. They had just shown us one of their most disrespectful signs by spitting on the lady in the group. I chose to treat them with respect as I said goodbye to them even though I wholeheartedly disagreed and was disgusted with their behavior.

After meeting with the prison psychologist and other officials for some time, we eventually made it through the prison gates and got back into our car outside the prison. There was a lot for us to process afterward. We learned that going through that narrow door had been one of the most dangerous moments of our visit. Prison stabbings usually happened in the prison when several folks gathered in a confined space like that one.

We also learned that spitting on me had been a clear message by the gang leaders and a proof-of-loyalty that the kids inside the room had to show to them. We discussed how those inmate kids had been taught that respect for life, property, family, or anything else was mandated by the gang leaders.

Needless to say, that is not *respect.* Respect stands on its own just like any of the other universal principles that Jesus taught. *No one* can determine when the principle applies or doesn't apply. Respect is a principle we live by that is true for anyone, anywhere, and at any time.

I'm sure that I am not alone when I say that I like other people to treat me with respect. Since that is how I would have them do to me, then I must do the same to them; treat them with respect. That is what I chose to do at the juvenile prison.

I must admit that there are times when this is not easy, but I've learned that treating others with respect can become easier as time goes on. It is another one of those habits that we need to implement in our lives one step at a time. It requires practice and patience. It seems difficult but it is not impossible if we ask the Lord to help us build that habit into our lives.

When we take inventory of all the great relationships we have with others, we can always find a couple of common denominators in each one of those relationships. First, we can quickly see that *respect* is the foundation on which those relationships were built. Second, we find that it took *time and effort* on their part and ours to build those relationships.

We only have great relationships with others when we treat them with respect. Abusive behavior on anyone's part can never lead to a great relationship with those who are the victims of that abuse. We can forgive abusive persons and strive to love them as God expects us to do but we will not have great relationships with them. Those types of relationships will always be strained and difficult.

Meaningful effort is also a necessary ingredient when we work at building great relationships with others. I know that some people seem to get new friends very quickly and without much effort. Although that is true for some very friendly individuals, I am talking about great relationships and not friendly acquaintances. A great relationship is the kind of relationship that we have with someone who we call in a time of crisis at 2 AM and he or she immediately jumps out of bed and comes to help us.

It takes respect and meaningful effort to build great relationships. That is the type of relationships that the Master expects us to have.[4] The choice is ours to make. As we put effort into our relationships, do we disagree agreeably, or do we disagree disrespectfully? Do we treat others with respect even in the face of persecution? Do we walk away the moment someone thinks and speaks differently than we do? The answer can be summarized in one single word. At the risk of sounding very corny here, I want to remind you of something that a great musical legend so beautifully sang for us: R-E-S-P-E-C-T![5] Thank you, Aretha Franklin, for reminding us of the Golden Rule.

Whether we are talking about a relationship with our spouse, children, parents, coworkers, or anyone else, we can accomplish so much more when we learn to treat every person with respect and put meaningful effort into it. This is exciting news! When we live by the principle of respect, we can go further in our life missions, accomplish more with our work, influence those around us for the better, and have great relationships with them. It is exciting indeed! That is the way it works when we climb with Jesus and obey his teachings; respect is the way of the Master.

* * *

TAKE AWAY- We don't have to see eye to eye to walk arm in arm.

GIVE AWAY- Do to others what you would have them do to you.

5

Integrity

"You're blessed when you get your inside world—your mind and heart—put right. Then you can see God in the outside world."[1]

I was 21 years old and so excited about going to a youth retreat in Casper, Wyoming. The reason for my excitement was that I had been invited to a church in Casper as the one and only speaker and I felt great. The retreat director, Ms. Marilyn, had scheduled me to speak at her youth camp several times over a period of five days.

I arrived in Casper and met the entire camp staff. Ms. Marilyn was also there and gave me full instructions for the week. She explained that she had selected a specific group of girls to stay with me in my cabin. She further explained that these girls were the most difficult group because of their behavior and pranks at previous youth camps. She expected me to keep them in line since they would be staying with me for the entire week.

I went to my cabin and met the girls. I could tell they were sizing me up as we were doing the usual introductions. I explained to them that I was the speaker for the retreat and that I wanted to make a deal with them. I caught their attention. I said to them, "I am going to ask you to behave in the best possible way throughout this week, no sneaking out of the cabin at night, no pranks on anyone during the day, and if you do this during the week, I promise you that I will help you pull the best prank ever on the last night of the camp. Deal?"

The girls were ecstatic! They could not believe the speaker would do something like that. So, the week started with a bang. I spoke several times. I met with the kids for small group discussions. We played games. It was a very good camp. Each morning during the camp, the counselors and staff met for prayer and planning. I was one of the counselors, so I was at each of the meetings. Ms. Marilyn praised me for the behavior of the girls in my cabin. She could not believe they were the same girls because of their good behavior.

Finally, the last night arrived. The girls wanted to know about the plan for that night. My 21-year-old maturity (or lack thereof) kicked in. I told them we would wait until everyone was sleep and then we would sneak out to the supplies cabin and get all the toilet paper we could find. I wanted to be honest and responsible, so I asked each of them to leave money on the toilet paper shelves to pay for the rolls we were taking away for our prank.

That night, we covered the entire camp with toilet paper. It looked like a snowstorm had hit the camp by the time we were done. The trees, cabins, picnic tables, and the entire campground were covered. We admired our handy work and quietly went back to our cabin. I then swore the girls to secrecy. No one was to find out who did it.

Early the next morning, the girls woke me up. They could not believe what had happened. We looked out the cabin window and saw that the camp was completely clean. No traces of toilet paper anywhere! We were bummed! All that work and nothing to show for it.

We went to breakfast. No one said anything about it. We could not understand it. We kept quiet about it though. All the kids went to pack their bags and I went to the counselors meeting. The tension was palpable at the meeting. Ms. Marilyn made it clear that no one would leave the retreat until the counselor responsible for the prank came forward. I thought to myself, "oh no, do we really have to do this?" The clock was ticking. No counselor said a word and neither did I. Ms. Marilyn then said, "Can you believe that whoever did this had the audacity to leave money on the shelves as if that would make it right?"

It seemed like an eternity while we waited in that meeting room. Lessons on integrity started flashing through my mind. Words about honesty from my parents, teachers, counselors, youth pastors and many others kept on screaming loud inside my head. Everyone at the meeting kept waiting. I don't know if you ever read Edgar Allan Poe's novel *The Tell-Tale Heart,*[2] but I could relate to the main character hearing the heart beats coming from under the floor. I could hear the toilet paper calling my name. Finally, I could not take it anymore and took a deep breath. I said, "It was me. My girls did it. I was with them."

The room got even more silent than before. The speaker had done it? Surely not! What a turn of events. I had to apologize to Ms. Marilyn and everyone else. I tried to reason my way through it but to no avail. I had done it and I needed to come clean. I knew better than that. A person of integrity does not hide things.

I don't even like to tell this story because it makes me relive those moments. But that lesson has served me well throughout my life. I strive to be a woman of integrity. If I realize I spoke something that was not true, I go back to whoever heard me and make it right. I work hard at living by the principle of integrity.

Integrity is such an all-encompassing universal principle. It is the quality of being honest, trustworthy, and of good character. **Integrity is doing what is right even when no one is looking.** Jesus told his climbing companions that doing what is right when no one is looking will bring about rewards in all areas of our lives.[3]

Reading this helps me realize that people living two thousand plus years ago, in another area of the world, were not much different than we are today. Many prefer to do what is right only when someone is looking in order to get credit for their deeds. But what really matters is what we do in secret.

I have a question for you: What does your secret life look like? We all need to know the answer to that question so we can work on the areas of our lives that need attention. Jesus also made it crystal clear that his climbing companions must not only hear his words but put them into practice if they want to have wisdom. It's impossible to be wise if we don't follow his teachings.[4]

Time and time again, every climbing companion of Jesus is reminded throughout the Christian scriptures that she or he is to be *pure in heart*. This tells me that we ought to have a steadfast adherence to universal principles without compromising one's wholeness regardless of what others expect. It is not about what people expect of us, it's about what the Master expects of us.

I really like the Latin words *sine cera*. The main reason I like them is because of their meaning when they are together. In ancient Rome, craftsmen would use those words to mean *without wax*. (Why without wax?) In those days, marble sculptures with imperfections or clay pots with minor cracks were patched up with wax and made to look whole again. Some people could be tricked into buying something that was not whole. Customers would find out that they had been tricked later when it was too late to get their money back. Sometimes, a strong light would be used to try to find any wax patches. So, it was common to ask craftsmen or street vendors, "Is this item *sine cera?*"

We need to ask ourselves the same question on a regular basis: are we *sine cera?* A derivative English word that applies here is the word *sincere.* Are we sincere and truthful with ourselves? Are we tricking ourselves into thinking that we are ok because of the things we try hard to do when everyone is looking? Can we hold our life to a light to see whether it is whole or if it has cracks in it?

Jesus' climbing companions need only ask him for the light that we can use to look deep within our hearts. He will reveal any cracks that need his healing touch. His healing is not done with wax; it is done with love and forgiveness. He wants us to be *pure in heart* and he will help us do it. We just need to ask for his help to be whole again.

Several years ago, a popular magazine polled a large number of people to find out who was the most influential Christian of all times. We all can guess that Jesus Christ made that list, but it was the apostle Paul who came up first on the list. We know what we know about the Christian faith in large part because of Paul's communication with various churches via the letters that he wrote to them. Many of those letters were written while he was in prison. Imagine what could have happened if he had never gone to prison; some of those powerful teachings would not have been recorded. Paul's positive influence can be felt across the world because of his integrity to the teachings of Jesus and his commitment to sharing those teachings with everyone.

Paul explained in one of his letters that God was creating a new humanity from climbing companions from all over the world through the reconciling work of the Messiah.[5] Then he asked them to practice purity in the way they lived and integrity in the way they handled all their relationships. He told them to *live as children of light.*[6] He encouraged them to expose everything by the light.[7] We need to always seek the light so we can be *pure in heart.*

Living by the principle of integrity offers us great benefits. *Moral authority* is one of those great benefits. More and more, we seem to fear that term in our culture today, but we shouldn't. Moral authority is a consistent alignment between our moral compass and our behaviors. It is just like a bridge that connects what we believe and say with what we do. I know that I will sometimes make a mistake but even in those times of failure, I can respond with integrity. When this alignment between what we say and what we do consistently takes place over a long period of time it gives us positive influence, credibility, and authority.

I frequently say to young people (it applies to us older people too) that our actions and lifestyle should never lead to the questioning of our integrity. Building moral authority takes years and it requires strong commitment. On the other hand, **moral authority is very fragile.** We can destroy our moral authority that has taken years to build with just one unwise decision. It also takes many years and it requires much love and grace to rebuild it if we ever compromise it with our actions. The rebuilding of moral authority is possible if we begin by acknowledging that we need God's forgiveness and strength for the journey. We must remember that forgiveness is instant, but re-establishing moral authority takes years and a lot of hard work.

I have been called for jury duty a few times in my life. Most of us cringe when that happens because of the amount of time it takes away from our daily schedule. I am no different but when I have to go, I remind myself that it is my responsibility to serve my community and that I ought to do it to the best of my ability. As you probably know, sometimes we must sit for hours waiting to be chosen for a trial. I have been fortunate that at times some judges gave us a chance to watch other trials while we waited.

When I had a chance to watch a trial, it was of great interest to see how people's reactions changed when they heard the testimony of someone accused of a crime and the accounts given by various witnesses. One always wonders who is telling the truth. But, the moment that one of the attorneys is able to establish that someone was lying about something of significance, people listening start to doubt other things that that individual has said or will say from there on out. You can watch that person's moral authority as it falls to pieces the moment that happens. It just takes one lie to turn the tables around on someone's testimony.

We all value integrity. The principle of integrity has been identified as the most desired trait in a leader. In virtually every survey of the desired qualities of a leader, integrity is identified more frequently than any other trait.[8]

The Christian scriptures also document endless examples of the importance of the principle of integrity. We can find scriptures that list people of integrity, people who compromised their moral authority and worked at regaining it, and people who chose to live a life without integrity and suffered the consequences.

I especially like the account of the Prime Minister of Egypt, a man of integrity named Joseph, which is documented in the Older Testament.[9] You may have read this account yourself or heard it used by someone as an illustration. Before his time as a Prime Minister, Joseph was a property manager for a wealthy man. This man's wife, probably accustomed to receiving male attention, noticed Joseph and asked him to go to bed with her. I think we should all memorize Joseph's response to her and use it if we ever find ourselves in a comparable tight spot. He said to her, "How then could I do such a wicked thing and sin against God?"[10] His integrity and commitment to do what was right in God's eyes gave Joseph the answer. His positive influence would be compromised if he did anything other than that. Joseph endured many challenges for a long time after this encounter. Each time he upheld his integrity. Maintaining integrity in different circumstances throughout his life resulted in Joseph being rewarded with the position of Prime Minister of Egypt.[11]

Another account that is documented in the Older Testament is that of a king who had it all but wanted to have just one more trophy. Many of us are very familiar with this account because it makes us seriously wonder why in the world he would do what I am about to describe to you. King David had it all by anyone's standards. He had fame, power, wealth, friends, and good looks to boot. But that was not enough. He compromised his moral authority by choosing to sleep with another man's wife and using his power to get away with it.[12]

God had given King David much up to that moment of his life. Unfortunately, King David learned the hard way what happens when we compromise our moral authority. He got his woman but lost the child she bore him, his kingdom, his friends, his influence, his wealth, and his health. The beautiful part of this story is that God allowed him to rebuild his moral authority. It took time and much sacrifice and suffering on the part of King David, but he eventually restored his moral authority.[13]

I wrote about the apostle Peter previously in this book. I like Peter because he seemed to be a man who made quick decisions and took action. Because I like Peter, I feel bad for him anytime I hear someone talking about his encounter with a certain rooster. In his typical style, Peter told Jesus that he was ready to go both to prison and to death for him.[14] Not long after that, Peter was weeping bitterly because he had denied that he even knew Jesus when suspected by others. Jesus had warned Peter that he did not yet have the strength of character needed to deal with what was about to happen.

Peter could have listened and asked Jesus to help him gain that strength but instead, he was bold and somewhat arrogant. Then, Jesus said to him, "I tell you the truth, Peter–this very night, before the rooster crows, you will deny three times that you even know me."[15] But there is a beautiful ending to Peter's story. We now remember Peter as the man on whom Jesus Christ bestowed the honor of carrying his legacy here on earth; the man on whom Jesus built his church.[16]

What can we learn from Joseph, David, and Peter? The first thing that comes to my mind is that life is not that much different today. We struggle with the same challenges, with the same behaviors, and with the same temptations. Our best weapon to help us deal with those challenges is the principle of integrity. One way to know if our actions and our lives demonstrate integrity is to ask ourselves a couple of simple questions:

- Would we be okay if our actions appeared on the front cover of our local newspaper?
- Would that newspaper display our name and actions as the story of a great humanitarian or an embarrassing scandal?

Walking tall with integrity is the best answer to those questions. I encourage you to do whatever it takes to build that habit into your life. Make a daily commitment that you want your house to be built on the rock, not on sand. I work hard at making that commitment each day. Be strong and follow the way of the Master. He is the only rock we need.

We all have influence over others whether we like it or not. The question is, "What kind of influence am I, positive or negative?" I venture to believe that you want to have a positive influence over others; so, do I. We can be a *positive influence* on others when we have chosen to be people of *integrity* and have made a *commitment* to do what is right.

A simple but powerful formula that I practice and teach others who want integrity to become a habit in their lives is this:

- **Decide:** decide what choice to make. Make your decision based on universal principles—principles that bring purpose, power, and peace.
- **Do:** take action based on the choice that you made. Don't listen to naysayers regardless of who they are.
- **Defend:** protect and defend the decision and action that you took. Stand strong when confronted by others.

Integrity is lived out when we make the commitment to be consistent with our actions across the board. Decide, do, and defend what is right time and time again. Remember that your walk talks and your talk talks, but your walk talks more than your talk talks. I encourage you to strive to have your words match your actions day after day so your testimony will always be strong and true.

* * *

TAKE AWAY - Integrity is built over a lifetime but can be destroyed in one moment with one decision.

GIVE AWAY - Your walk talks and your talk talks, but your walk talks more than your talk talks.

6

Self-Control

"Blessed are the gentle, for they shall inherit the earth."[1]

I will always remember a somewhat upsetting discussion that I had with a young man (well, he was young back then) while I attended seminary classes in the Midwest. It was a typical classroom session and our professor was discussing potential ministry challenges that we could all face. Then, the professor brought up the topic of women in ministry. The men in the class engaged quite energetically in that discussion. Many views of women in ministry were thrown around as the discussion evolved. I was quietly listening to those men when the professor interrupted and said, "Lori, you are the only woman in this class. Why don't you tell us your view of women in ministry?"

I was ready to speak my mind (not a big surprise to anyone who knows me). I enthusiastically shared my views and tried to help the men see different perspectives. Just as I was finishing what I thought was a great defense on the topic, one of the men in the class said loud enough for everyone to hear, "If God could use Balaam's donkey, I am sure he could use women in ministry, right

Lori?" His timing was perfect, and the class had a good laugh. I was taken aback by his comment. He had chosen to use a more vulgar name for the donkey in his comment. I responded immediately to him, "It takes one to know one!" The class oohed and laughed a bit more. The professor did not comment one way or the other on the exchange that had just taken place. He ended the discussion and wrapped up the class for the day.

"Balaam's *donkey*, are you kidding me?" The thought kept on repeating inside my head as I went to work. I was working full-time at a local church. It was hard to erase that comment from my mind (it still pops into my mind now and then). A couple of months later our senior pastor announced that he wanted to introduce us to someone who was applying for one of the open ministry positions at the church. To my surprise, in walked the same guy who had called me a donkey in class.

He walked head tall and ready to make a good impression. He looked around the circle and smiled at each of the staff members until he saw me sitting there. I knew what he was thinking, and I also knew that revenge was within my reach. The interview started with the senior pastor asking some questions and our candidate doing the best he could to give the most eloquent answers. When all the questions had been asked, our pastor asked if any of us knew the candidate from before. I was the only one who did; I raised my hand.

The pastor was delighted that someone could give a personal recommendation on this guy. He asked my opinion of the candidate. As you may imagine, my feelings and emotions had been very active during the interview. I thought of the many things that I could say when the opportunity presented itself.

Here it was! My opportunity to set the record straight with this *dude* had been given to me on a silver platter. I was ready to speak but something didn't feel quite right. I paused and silently said to myself, "Lord, what is the right thing to do?" I was asking the Lord whether I needed to follow the way of the world or the way of the Master. The answer was clear, but I sure didn't like it. I had prepared such a good speech in my mind, but it looked like that speech would never see the light of day.

The senior pastor said, "C'mon Lori, give us your thoughts on the candidate."

I said, "He is very strong in his opinions, his beliefs, and his ideas." I paused and swallowed hard; then, I continued, "While I may not agree with all of his opinions and beliefs ... I do believe that he would make a great staff member."

I can't remember much after that. The pastor eventually ended the meeting and we all walked out. I went to the drinking fountain and my classmate followed me there. He said, "Thank you, Lori. I know you could have kept me from getting this job."

I said, "I know but I decided not to be a *donkey*." (One of the few times in my life when I saw fit to use a more vulgar term for a donkey.)

He was hired and he indeed made a great staff member. We ended up working well together. It was years later after I had moved to another city that my brother, Jerry, told me about an informal discussion he overheard at a conference. The discussion was on the topic of women in ministry. My brother said that one of the men engaged in the discussion had said, "I used to think like you do but I now know that women in ministry can be powerful and effective instruments of God. I worked with a woman in ministry named Lori Salierno and she changed my mind." These words came from the very same but now enlightened *dude* from long ago.

Oh, the power of the universal principle of self-control! We, climbing companions of Jesus, need to exercise self-control. It is not an option; it's a requirement. "Blessed are the gentle, for they shall inherit the earth."[2] That is quite a promise Jesus made to us. He was not asking us to be *doormats* and let everyone figuratively step all over us. **He asked us to be gentle and keep our strength under control.** Jesus was also telling us that we would be rewarded here on earth for our gentle strength. It takes both strength and discipline in order for us to exercise the principle of self-control.

Hearing my friend's comment after so many years was truly a reward here on earth. To know that he went on to be a strong climbing companion of Jesus and be a positive influence on young women who were thinking of, or working in, Christian ministry was my reward.

I think it is safe to say that most of us like to be in control. We want to *be the boss* of our own decisions, actions, schedules, etc. I think it is so much better when we have control of our *self* instead of having others control our *self*. Why would I want to give others control over my life? No way—I would never want to.

It is much better when we first think through our decisions before we respond instead of quickly reacting to a person or situation. If we react without thinking, we are letting our emotions control our decisions and, in doing so, we are allowing others to negatively influence our emotions with their harsh words or hurtful actions. Every time we let our feelings and emotions take over, we end up *reacting* instead of *responding*.

It takes practice to develop the discipline of responding instead of reacting. When I mentor young people, I ask them to practice with little things such as eating a fruit instead of a donut; or, walking from the end of the parking lot to a store instead of parking right in front of it; or, turning the TV off for one hour and picking up a good book to read instead. These are things that we know are good for us but that we just don't want to do. Our emotions say, "eat the donut," "don't park so far away," and "watch TV all night." All the while, our rational thinking says something different. Each time we choose the better option in these little things is another time when we have given ourselves a dose of strength which will eventually help us be successful at much bigger things.

The discipline of responding versus reacting is crucial when we deal with people who are more difficult than the average person. These are the people who know how to push our buttons. Our emotions go on high alert when we encounter them. We can hear our emotions screaming things like "hang up on her" or "talk behind his back" or "give them the silent treatment." Instead of our emotions, our mind must be on high alert.

A climbing companion of Jesus who strives to have self-control in all areas of her or his life must think before responding to those sorts of people. We must practice saying things like, "I want to think about it before we continue this discussion" or "I'm not going to say something now that I wouldn't say in front of him" or "I am not ready to give an opinion at this time."

Self-control is about leading self. It's interesting that we sometimes find out that leading others is easier than leading self. In order to lead ourselves, we need to learn to navigate the highs of life with the same strength as we navigate the lows. Sometimes we face some very serious lows and we don't feel strong enough to get past them. That is why I always suggest having an accountability partner(s).

I have personally seen the value of having such persons in my life. Some people think of their accountability partner as those who enjoy the same social activities, but the accountability relationship needs to be much more formal than that. Enjoying social times together is fine but when accountability meetings take place, it's serious business. We must have a clear understanding of how we will hold each other accountable.

Our accountability partner(s) also need to know our weak areas and our most difficult temptations. We must be willing to ask each other tough questions that can help us find out what areas of our life we need to work on next. Accountability is a key ingredient as we develop the discipline of leading self.

Accountability partner(s) are such a great help as we practice the discipline of responding versus reacting. For them to help us, we have to make sure that our accountability partner(s) know the profile of those individuals with whom we have challenges. They also should ask us questions about what we are doing to deal with those individuals. Exchanging this information will help us process the difficult emotions, both emotionally and intellectually, that we experience when we deal with those individuals. Having our accountability partner(s) ask us questions and role play scenarios prepare us to respond and not react in the future.

Perhaps, the most prolific of Jesus's early climbing companions was the apostle Paul. He left a wealth of powerful instructions in his many letters to churches. The leaders of those early churches would ask Paul to come to their city and bring clarity to certain ideas or beliefs. One of those early churches, in the wealthy and cosmopolitan city of Corinth, sent a letter with key questions to the apostle Paul.

In Paul's reply to the Corinthian church, he explained to them that all the ministry work that they were doing in the name of Jesus was very important and that it would not be wasted in

God's economy. Paul gave them some practical advice on how to live their lives while they were doing their ministry work. He knew that lack of self-control would have a negative impact on their mission. So, he explained to them (and to us) that whenever they were not strong enough to overcome their temptations, God would be there to give them (and us) a way out![3]

That is such great news! We, climbing companions, ought to work hard at developing our self-control but if we ever find ourselves in a situation that goes beyond what we can handle, the Lord will step in and help us. I don't know about you but learning this was like a huge Christmas present for me. I know that developing self-control is very difficult at times. But we know that if we work hard to do our best, he will then do the rest. That is almost too good to be true! It is amazingly good and very reassuring. That is the way of the Master.

Not long ago, I told José that I was ready to buy a new car. He was surprised and wanted to know what was wrong with my current vehicle. He takes pride in helping me have a safe and reliable car, so he was curious about what was wrong with my car. I told him, "There is nothing wrong with it."

He looked puzzled and said, "Sorry, I misunderstood you. I thought you said you wanted a *new* car but what you said was that you wanted something new for your car. Are you talking about that XM radio you talked about?"

I make quick decisions on most things; I had decided that morning that it was time for a new car. So, I said to him, "No, you heard me right the first time. I want to buy a new car. There is nothing wrong with my current 17-year old car but it's time to retire it. It is old and retirement is in its very near future."

"Lori, cars don't need to retire. We get rid of them when they don't work anymore. You are trying to be funny, right?"

"I am not sure how to tell you that I am serious. I decided that I want to buy a new car and put this perfectly running car out to pasture. Or, you can sell it if you want to."

Well, the conversation ended up being much longer than what I thought was necessary. José had difficulty grasping the concept of replacing a car that is in perfect running shape. On the other hand, it made perfect sense to me. We talked some more, and the conversation shifted towards the amount of money that we would need to spend to buy a new car.

I started looking at the situation from the money angle and I decided that I needed to think about my decision a little more. We postponed our conversation for a couple of days. I set some time aside to think about the car issue. Later, something occurred to me, was I suffering from "instant gratification-itis"? Instant gratification says, "You have to have it right now no matter what." Self-control says, "Let's put this thought to the test."

I decided that I needed to practice what I preach. Throughout my life, I have used a self-control test that is simple yet extremely effective. It helps anyone with responding instead of reacting to an idea, a situation, or a confrontation. I encourage you to add this test to your decision-making process:

- Does this _____ please and glorify God?
- Does this _____ add value to my or someone else's life?
- Is this _____ absolutely necessary?

You probably guessed what my answer was after I put the new car issue to the test. No, it is not time for me to buy a new car. (I almost felt that I had to go back to my car and ask it not to be mad at me for wanting to retire it.) José and I had a follow-up discussion. We both agreed that we could wait until we are ready to make the financial investment and get a new car for me.

Instant gratification has become so much a part of our culture that we almost feel as if it is a *right*. It is not! We can wait. Our world does not end when we wait. Our old cars get us where we need to go. Our old houses continue to provide shelter. Rational thinking must prevail. Good decisions make life so much better in the long run. Living by the principle of self-control does produce great rewards.

I want to encourage you to read and digest the steps listed below as you continue developing the habit of self-control and leading self. These steps have been of great help to me and many others that I have mentored through the years. These four steps may seem like a lot of work at first, but I assure you that they can easily become part of your daily life if you give them a chance.

1. Decide to be guided and motivated by God's Spirit. Read through the book of Galatians, chapter 5, verses 16 through 26 in the Newer Testament. There you will find an abundantly clear definition of what it means to be guided by God's Spirit. I guarantee that reading through it will not disappoint. It is the way of the Master.

2. Identify and write down any temptations in your life that could cause you to react and do something harmful instead of responding. By admitting that these temptations conflict with the way of the Master, you are on your way to staying in step with God's Spirit.

3. Choose a strong accountability partner(s) who can be confidential. Agree with each other that you will use step one above as your one and only constitution for accountability. Next, exchange with each other the list you created in step

two above. It is important that both of you be committed to being Jesus' climbing companions.

4. Pray that God's Spirit will give you the desire to want to make positive changes in your life based on what you have learned in steps one, two, and three above. Please remember that these changes will serve you very well and that they will also serve the Kingdom of God here on earth.

The grandfather of one of our friends had a saying about self-control. His saying was, "It has been said that we need to count until 10 before we respond. I have chosen to count until 20." What a wise suggestion we can all use. **I encourage you to practice counting until 10 and then until 20 before you respond to the challenges that life may present you.** May the universal principle of self-control help you enjoy a superior way of life. That is the way of the Master.

* * *

TAKE AWAY: Develop the discipline of responding instead of reacting.

GIVE AWAY: Focus on what you will gain not what you will lose when exercising self-control.

7

Courage

*"Blessed are those who are persecuted because of righteous-
ness, for theirs is the kingdom of heaven."*[1]

The scenery was breathtaking as we made our way along the well-marked trail. We knew we would soon see something quite extraordinary, but we had to walk carefully so we would not slip on the wet path. Our anticipation kept on building up with every step we took. A few minutes later, we got to the spot that the owner of the bed-and-breakfast where we had stayed the night before told us about. José and I stood there in awe.

Unlike what happens when we stand in an open field on a rainy day, the water vapor at that spot seemed to magically appear from everywhere and our clothes were drenched within a few moments. It also seemed as if some invisible hand had turned up the volume on some gigantic speakers; the immense roaring sound was now louder than before. I wiped the water off my eyes to try to get a better view of the majestic beauty before me.

We were standing in front of one of the world's most astonishing vistas, "The Thundering Smoke,"[2] which is more commonly known as Victoria Falls.

Victoria Falls is twice the size of our own Niagara Falls. It is located at the border of Zambia and Zimbabwe where the Zambezi River is 5,000 feet wide. While there, we learned that the impressive river descends 355 feet to the bottom of the falls at the astonishing rate of 33,000 cubic feet per second. That is a whole lot of water crashing down into the bottom of that precipice. As I soaked in the experience that morning, I came to appreciate these words in a new and inspiring way: "It was my hand that laid the foundations of the earth, my right hand that spread out the heavens above. When I call out the stars, they all appear in order."[3] Something as extraordinarily beautiful as Victoria Falls must have been brought forth by an amazing creator.

When we eventually walked away from that marvelous natural wonder, I was intrigued by the fact that it is better known to most of us by its English name. I had read about missionary-explorer David Livingstone on occasions throughout my life but his connection to Victoria Falls was somewhat unknown to me.

José and I made it a point to learn about David Livingstone as much as we could while we were in Zimbabwe. We talked with locals and traveled to neighboring Zambia to visit a museum about his life in the city that bears his name right next to Victoria Falls—the city of Livingstone. The more that we asked and learned about David Livingstone, the more we kept on hearing the words *Christ-follower*, *adventuresome,* and *courageous* to describe him.

We learned that Livingstone was born in Scotland. By the young age of 28, he had made his way to South Africa with the eager desire to share the gospel of Jesus Christ with those who had not yet heard it. When he arrived in Africa, the continent was as unknown to the civilized world as outer space. Livingstone's adventuresome spirit and unconventional ministry approach propelled him to launch some of the most dangerous explorations of the nineteenth century. His godly mission gave him the courage to take on the risks of each of his journeys. In 1853, Livingstone ventured into what is today known as the country of Namibia with the vision to create what he called "God's Highway" for the purpose of bringing Christianity and civilization to those unreached people.

During one of his trips deep into the bush of that part of the African continent, he and his Makololo warrior companions reached what the natives called Mosioatunya—The Thundering Smoke. He called it "the most wonderful sight I had seen in Africa" and later re-christened it in honor of Queen Victoria.

Each step Livingstone took for the cause of Christ was filled with courage. I began to wonder what it was that gave Livingstone such courage. Was he born courageous or was he trained by his parents to be courageous? How does a person have the courage to venture into the unknown wilderness without knowledge of language or terrain for months at a time? Merriam-Webster's dictionary gives us a partial answer to that question. It gives the definition of courage as the "mental or moral strength to venture, persevere, and withstand danger, fear, or difficulty."

Others define courage as an attitude of confidence that seizes opportunities that benefit humanity even when enormous risks are involved. Studying courageous people such as David Livingstone and many others like him throughout history, I see courage as the merging of two valuable traits in our lives: having the *confidence* to overcome our fears and taking *heroic risks* so we can achieve our goals and dreams. Also, I see courage as standing up for or defending a just cause. When we go about purposely doing what we know to be right, we gain the right measure of confidence that helps us master our fears. Notice that I didn't say eliminate our fears. **We cannot erase our fears, but we can rule over them.**

There are countless examples of courageous deeds done by many different individuals in the Christian scriptures. We read about a young man by the name of Daniel who had to endure jealousy and persecution because he lived a godly life; he had the courage to face punishment and potential death in a lion's den because of his faith.[4] We also learn that three young men, Shadrach, Meshach, and Abednego—were courageous when they were maliciously accused of being disrespectful to the king. Soldiers threw them into a burning furnace because of their faith.[5] In these stories, we are happy to see that their commitment to do what was right in the eyes of God gave them much needed courage and they were protected from death.

We also read the story of a woman, a prostitute no less, who hid two spies, tossed a red ribbon outside of her window as a signal, and gained safety and security for her whole family with her courageous act of insubordination against her government.[6] We see how her desire to live a godly life gave her the courage to act boldly.

There is also the story of Puah and Shiphrah, the often-forgotten midwives who hid and prevented the murder of innocent Hebrew babies after being ordered by government decree that they ought to kill every male baby upon their birth. These two women had the courage to disobey an evil law and do what was right because they feared God and wanted his blessings. They were given their own families as a reward for their faith and courage.[7]

What is the common denominator among those stories from long ago and similar ones from recent times? The Lord Jesus Christ explained the common denominator to his climbing companions when he walked on this earth. He said, "Blessed are those who are persecuted for righteousness' sake, for theirs is the kingdom of heaven."[8]

The Master wanted us to know that there is a high likelihood that we will be persecuted when we do what is right. We must build up our courage so we can stand firm in the face of persecution. The universal principle of courage carries a warning for all climbing companions of Jesus; this warning was just as true 2,000 years ago as it is today. The warning tells us that once someone chooses not to live by worldly standards, he or she becomes a target of the enemy and must be eliminated. However, we ought to know that those who make the choice to live by God's universal principles and have the courage to stand firm by them will be handsomely rewarded in heaven.

What about now though? We see that we will be rewarded in heaven but what happens in the here and now? After all, we like rewards for doing good things. The reality is that we have not been given the promise of rewards here on earth for being courageous in the face of persecution. What we have been given is the promise of help when we go through persecution. God assured us he would never leave us alone or let us down. This ought to give us courage just like it did to each of those characters in those stories. After all, if God is there with me, "I'm fearless no matter what. Who or what can get to me?"[9]

So, courage is truly an attitude of confidence. That confidence comes from knowing we will never be left alone by God. Furthermore, Jesus also told us that we are *blessed* when we have the courage to face persecution for what is right. I like that a lot and

I hope you do, too! Confidence gives us the strength to take on heroic risks so that our mission and purpose on this earth can become a reality in our lifetime.

We all have been previously stamped with a life purpose.[10] We must get ready and take on whatever risk is necessary to go forward and accomplish that purpose. Discovering our God-given purpose helps us muster the courage that we need to overcome our fears and do the right thing. We will face opposition and persecution at times, but our resolve needs to remain intact. I encourage you to pray frequently for that resolve.

The Older Testament of the Christian scriptures contains what some traditions call the Book of Reigns. This book was one long book that ended up being divided into two and later into four books so it would fit onto ancient scrolls. Those are known as 1 and 2 Samuel and 1 and 2 Kings. The Book of Reigns describes in detail many aspects of the lives of King Saul and King David and the rest of the Israelite monarchy from beginning to end. One story in that book that has captivated millions of people throughout history is the one about King David as a young boy.

Through a sequence of unusual events, young David found himself without much fighting gear and facing a very large soldier named Goliath who was determined to kill him. Young David's narrative highlights a couple of steps that can be very useful to us thousands of years later as we prepare ourselves to face our own challenges and be people of courage.

David was certainly a person of courage even at an early age. We read the story and find out that he accepted the challenge and ran toward the battle line to meet his adversary. David did not hold back and did not try to find excuses or run away when the going got tough.

We also read that David stood firm against the opposition. He spoke out with confidence and stood firm in the face of danger. Just reading his words can give us courage: "This day the Lord will deliver you into my hands, and I'll strike you down and cut off your head."[11]

Lastly, we find out that David also knew how to prepare for victory. It is obvious that he already knew that God was enough. David made it clear that it was not the first time he had faced impossible challenges and that he had come out victorious each of those previous times.

To bring down the Goliaths in our lives, we must become courageous climbing companions. Courageous climbing companions have a firmness of spirit that comes from saying *yes* to the challenge. The dark forces of evil in the spiritual world have a very difficult time stopping the courageous climbing companions who fear nothing but Christ himself and who consistently run toward the challenge set before them.

We frequently give power to the wrong things in our lives which can, in turn, make us weak and ineffective. A couple of things that may hold us back are the fear of physical harm and the fear of what others think of us. These are real fears that can debilitate us and make us ineffective to the point of making us physically ill.

If we give a lot of power to the fear of physical harm, we will stop ourselves from going to places of great need and doing something of great significance because physical harm or death may be a possibility. If we give a lot of power to what others think of us, we may stop ourselves from doing something that is pleasing to God hoping that others will have a good opinion of us.

In order to have the courage to pursue our purpose in life and quit giving power over us to the wrong things in our

lives, we need to change our focus. We do that by focusing on what the outcome will be if we go forward with our mission despite our fears. We cannot help changing lives for the better if the focus is our fears.

To quit giving power over us to the wrong things, we can also use our fears to our advantage. Some people choose to go forward despite their fears while others do not. Those who go forward have learned to recognize that most of the fears that hold us back are a state of mind with no logical explanation. They take those fears as a sign that what they are about to do is of great significance and their fear has simply confirmed it. We can allow our fears to either motivate or paralyze us. If we don't learn to conquer our fears, then they will conquer us.

I love the quote defining courage that became widely circulated throughout the internet. It was first used by a police superintendent at a memorial ceremony for a fallen police officer in the year 2002. It is a quote from a fellow by the name of Ambrose Redmoon that says, "Courage is not the absence of fear, but rather the judgment that something else is more important than one's fear."

The Apostle Paul is a great example to us of a person who did not give power to the fear of physical harm, even death, or any other fear. He knew there was something else that was more important than his fear. Survival was not his ultimate goal. The way he lived his life seemed to scream, "I don't have to survive!" He was the one who penned the verse that has given strong encouragement to many who grieve loved ones after they are no longer in this world: "For to me, living means living for Christ, and dying is even better."[12]

You probably have faced serious challenges of your own. How did you navigate through them? Did you conquer your fears and rise above your challenges? Whether your answer is *yes* or *no*, what did you learn from it? Those experiences can contribute to our preparation so we can get stronger and be ready to take the challenges which are sure to come.

I encourage you to develop the habit of doing those things which cause you to be fearful but that you know will please Jesus when you do them. If you don't see yourself as a courageous person, start with small things and over time, build up to bigger things. That is what preparation is all about. Put effort into building up your confidence, too. A simple but very effective confidence-building exercise is to repeat scriptures daily that remind you that God has a purpose for your life.

While we were in Zimbabwe, José and I decided that we wanted to see Victoria Falls a second time. We chose to walk there instead of taking a taxi. My husband, in whom I am well pleased, but who almost never wants to take the road most traveled, decided that we needed to take a shortcut through the bush as we made our way to the falls instead of walking along the paved road. I was somewhat skeptical about taking that dirt path, but he was so excited about walking through the real African bush that I decided to go along with the idea. We walked for a while until we got to a place where we had to climb down an old and rusty maintenance ladder that was hanging from a side of a hill. At the bottom of the ladder, we arrived at a spot where we could see a whole different view of Victoria Falls. We could see the massive flow of water after it had splashed at the bottom of the falls. What a great spectacle!

We stood there for a while and took some pictures. Then, we climbed back up the rusty and now shaky ladder and once at the top, started our trek back on the dirt trail. We had walked for a while when we spotted some locals ahead of us waving frantically.

They had been walking towards us but had stopped and were pointing towards some trees. We walked a bit closer to them and could now understand what they were trying to tell us. There was apparently some beast in the thick bush on the edge of the trail and these people were telling us to turn back the way we came. They turned around and went back the way they came. I quickly turned to walk away in the opposite direction, but José said, "Wait a minute. We don't know what is in the bush. Let's go and check it out so we know what those locals were all upset about."

I responded, "Seriously, you heard from people who live here that we need to get away. They ran away, but you rather go and check it out! You aren't serious, are you?"

He calmly said, "Lori, how many times in our lives do we get to walk in the African bush? And on top of that, how many times do we get the chance to see real wildlife up close and personal! C'mon how bad can it be?"

With that, he started walking towards the part of the trail the locals had warned us about. I told him I was not sure it was wise (actually, I was sure it was not at all wise!), but as he walked, I decided to go along with him. Pretty soon, we got to the spot and found the source of the commotion. A huge elephant was standing on the edge of the trail and it turned its head towards us. José took another step and the elephant started a lot of ear flapping, head shaking, and loud trumpeting. We turned back and ran as fast as we could. There we met up with another couple of locals who were coming up behind us on the trail. We told them about the elephant and they immediately went in the opposite direction. At this point, José said, "We have to go back and get a picture!"

Only one word came out of my mouth (kind of unusual for me),

"Whaaaaat?"

José started walking back to the elephant and said, "C'mon Lori, just one picture ... or you can stay back there, and I will be right back."

"What? Leave me alone here? No way. I'm coming with you."

We got back to the elephant again. This time, it looked more irritated than before. It quickly did another mock charge and away we went running again. I've heard of people running with the bulls in Pamplona, Spain and I always wondered why anybody would want to do that. But here I was running from an elephant in the middle of the African bush.

Our third attempt yielded the same results and I am glad we were able to go home after that. We eventually got back to our bed-and-breakfast in the late afternoon. It turned out to be a very fun day (including the elephant part but don't tell José I said that). At the B&B I asked him, "Why did you want to do that? It was dangerous."

As he smiled, he said, "We're always talking and teaching about *courage*. So, here was the perfect opportunity to put it into practice!"

I am glad he was joking because he knows, just as much as I do, that what we did was *not* courage. Courage is a combination of confidence and heroic risk. This elephant stunt was not a heroic risk, instead, it was risky behavior. Those two expressions sound similar but there is a big difference. A heroic risk is doing something that will usually have an element of danger, but its outcome will be of benefit to humanity in some way. Risky behavior, on the other hand, exposes us to danger without any purpose and with potentially negative consequences.

As we teach children and young adults about courage, we must help them understand what heroic risk really means. Most of them love to take risks on a regular basis. Most of us (although not all of us) grow out of it as we get older. Young people need to understand that taking a risk to benefit others is the right thing to do. Risky behavior on the other hand, well, it's just plain crazy (and we could use other less eloquent words here).

There are people around us who display courage and are quick to engage in heroic risk. We can use these people as role models for our children. There are firefighters, law enforcement personnel, soldiers, teachers, doctors, preachers, and many more who exemplify the universal principle of courage. We all get opportunities to be courageous as we go about our daily lives and perform the duties required within our own specialized fields.

The organization I am privileged to lead is full of courageous people who get up each day to follow the calling to change the lives of kids who are in trouble. They have chosen to be mentors. Some of them overcome the fear of speaking in public because they know that helping kids is more important than their fear. Others walk into public high school campuses even though they may be fearful about being there. We are very thankful for each one of our courageous mentors. Courageous climbing companions stand up for what they believe in and what is right even if nobody else is standing at all.

There are also many examples of courageous people from old and recent history. As parents or mentors, we need to help our children learn about some of those heroes. We need to place books in our children's hands that have pictures and quotes from those heroes. We need to explain to them what made those individuals heroes and what challenges they had to face in their lifetime. There are well-known and not-so-well-known heroes who made history by being courageous people such as Joan of Arc, Roy Benavidez, Thich Quang Duc, Mahatma Gandhi, Nelson

Mandela, Rosa Parks, Ronald Reagan, George Washington, and the list goes on.

I like this quote from Ralph Waldo Emerson, "A hero is no braver than an ordinary man, but he is brave five minutes longer." Most of the time, that is what it takes for us to bring about change or benefit humanity. We need to give less priority to our fears and stay at our mission just a little while longer.

As climbing companions of Jesus, we must learn to appropriate the courage that is already ours. We need that courage to become warriors who fight the good fight. It is like going to the bank to appropriate money that we have previously deposited. Since that money is ours, we just need to take it. Courage comes to us from God as we embark on what he has called us to do. He calls us to do what pleases him and he will give us the strength to get it done.

Our job is to claim the courage which God has given us and is already ours. The process begins by taking one step followed by another and followed by another. As climbing companions, we are called to be courageous warriors who fix our thoughts, fight, and defend what is true, honorable, right, pure, lovely, admirable, excellent, and worthy of praise.[13]

I mentioned Ambrose Redmoon's quote on courage earlier in this chapter. I want to leave you with a more comprehensive written piece from this little-known author who did not have anything formally published but whose name has gone around the world via the internet with his definition of courage:

> *As a real, live, initiated, trained, experienced, traditional, hereditary warrior with thirty-seven body scars and a trophy or two on my belt, I find such expressions as "peaceful warrior" offensive, trivializing, and insulting. "Peaceful*

warrior" *is far more than a contradiction in terms. The*
function of a warrior is to eliminate an exterior enemy
presence. Cowardice is a serious vice. Courage is not the
absence of fear, but rather the judgment that something else
is more important than one's fear. The timid presume it is
lack of fear that allows the brave to act when the timid do
not. But to take action when one is not afraid is easy. To
refrain when afraid is also easy. To take action regardless of
fear is brave.[14]

* * *

TAKE AWAY: We must accept the challenge, stand firm against
opposition and prepare for victory in order to bring down the
giants in our lives and in the lives of those whom we help.

GIVE AWAY: Taking heroic risks and being courageous to help
others is the right thing to do.

8

Excellence

"Blessed are those who hunger and thirst for righteousness,
for they shall be satisfied."[1]

My husband often says he does not have many friends. This is either a joke or he lacks self-awareness because everywhere he goes, he finds people he knows. Anytime he says that I ask him, "What about your best friend Barry?" He simply smiles. Barry and José have known each other since they were very young. When José first introduced me to Barry, he told me that I would probably run into him at an airport someplace because he was a commercial pilot. According to José, his friend has had a love and passion for aviation his whole life. Barry received his undergraduate degree in Aeronautical Science and earned his pilot's private, multi-engine, and instrument ratings while in college.

After college, Barry's passion for flying took him to various places around the U.S. where he worked as a commercial pilot for smaller airlines. He gained experience by logging flight hours in the summer heat of Florida and in the cold winters of Vermont.

He pursued aviation with passion and determination. José often tells me that one would be hard pressed to find a better pilot than Barry.

After a few years of flying for various airlines, Barry took a job as a flight engineer with a large U.S.-based airline. At this airline, he worked hard at gaining knowledge and experience, and later took a job as a flight instructor. That was many years ago. During that season of Barry's life, I founded a non-profit organization with the express purpose of mentoring kids in public high schools. José and Barry took some of those kids, who were on the verge of dropping out of school and inspired them to pursue higher education by having them fly real Boeing 727 flight simulators. What a treat that was for those high school students and a great way to help them create a new narrative for their life.

Barry tells many interesting and, at times, very humorous stories about things that have happened to him while flying airplanes around the world. I remember the time he told us about helping a lady out of the airplane's restroom because she had gotten suctioned to the toilet seat after flushing it (how embarrassing that must have been).

José and I went out to dinner with Barry and his wife. During that dinner, I asked Barry to tell us one of his flying stories. He told us a story that turned out to be of great interest to me. He talked about a time when he was ready to take off from a South American airport and found a problem with a component in the airplane that he was about to fly. He was a first-officer (copilot) at that time. He said he was doing his pre-flight routine when he encountered that issue with the airplane.

As expected, Barry brought the issue up to the captain and recommended that they wait until someone in maintenance could figure out what needed to be done to correct the problem.

The captain was apparently not interested in waiting and felt comfortable flying back to the U.S. using a backup system. He wanted to leave on time and get home on time. He told Barry that they needed to take off and that they would make sure the plane would go into maintenance once they arrived at the U.S.

Barry had a decision to make. He would either go along with the captain's decision in order to avoid a confrontation or disagree with the captain's decision by holding the flight back at that airport. He chose the latter. Since they were at an airport that lacked a reliable aircraft maintenance crew, Barry decided to communicate with flight operations in the U.S. and wait for their response regardless of the captain's objections.

Barry's commitment to the principle of excellence would not allow him to do just *good enough* work. He knew that the backup system would probably work good enough to get them home but what if that system was to fail during the flight. José and I were very interested in hearing what Barry's thought process had been throughout the whole situation. Moments like this happen in every one of our lives. Those critical moments occur when our character and commitment to principle-based living is tested. Our friend Barry was tested that day but his commitment to high standards guided him to choose the high road. He ended up having to deal with a difficult captain but that was still better than compromising his commitment to the principle of excellence.

Most of us do not have to worry about the safety of a couple of hundred passengers on a commercial flight when we make our decisions. However, our daily decisions do have consequences even when they are not about life or death. Each decision we make is a reflection of our character. More importantly, each decision we make may be an example of what to do or what not to do for those who may be watching us. Our own children or the children of others in our communities are watching us and often emulating what we do. What kind of an example to young people do we want to be? I am quite sure that you and I want to be good examples to children (and adults) on how to live a principled life. Am I right?

It took Barry many years to become the pilot he is today. We know that the principle of excellence does not accidentally happen. It is the result of continuous and often arduous effort on our part. Excellence is the direct result of both a *passion* for something that is worth doing and the continuous *pursuit of knowledge*. **Excellence keeps us striving for the best and does not allow one to settle for what is average.**

We can clearly see *passion* in our lives when we find ourselves working at something that we love and not allowing anything to get in our way. Some of us are passionate about sharing our faith, practicing a particular art form, helping young people become responsible citizens, caring about the environment, or anything else you can name.

It is good for us to remind ourselves of the fact that obstacles will present themselves in our daily lives and try to separate us from our passion, but we need to be strong and find ways to overcome them. Our passion for a worthwhile cause can give us the strength to overcome those difficult obstacles that we may find on our way to reach our hopes and dreams.

The *pursuit of knowledge* is another important ingredient as we strive to be people of excellence. Pursuing knowledge is a deliberate effort at seeking to gain facts and truths through education and experiences in order to achieve something of significance. Many of the people I know decided not to pursue knowledge as soon as they earned their high school diploma. Others seem to have stopped when they completed their college degree. Yet for those people who live by the principle of excellence, the pursuit of knowledge never seems to end. For this last group, learning is not confined to a specific degree, rather it is a lifelong commitment. It is only through the pursuit of knowledge that we can gain the truths that we need to accomplish our purpose in life.

I hope you are the kind of person who wants to lead a life that makes a positive difference in this world. If you are not currently enrolled in school, you can attend seminars, listen to educational podcasts or Ted Talks, join a book club, learn a new skill at a local technical college, or spend time with someone you have appointed as your mentor. The options for learning are endless.

The Messiah taught his climbing companions long ago about the things they ought to pursue and he told them, "Blessed are those who hunger and thirst for righteousness, for they shall be satisfied."[2] He used very descriptive language to express what he wanted his companions to understand. He referred to our two most common daily appetites: hunger and thirst. Put this book down and take a few moments to think about the last time you were truly hungry or thirsty. Well? What did you think about? I'm almost sure that the only thing you thought about was the food that you would soon eat or the cold and satisfying drink that you would soon drink.

It is almost as if nothing else matters when we are *really* hungry or thirsty; those desires seem to consume us until the moment when we can satisfy them. You may even start feeling hungry or thirsty right now just by thinking of that last time when you had those strong feelings of hunger or thirst. I assume that Jesus used that reference so we all can understand the kind of passionate appetite that he expects us to have for what is right. When we read those words that he shared long ago, we see that he wants his climbing companions to passionately desire what is right.

How do we make sure that we passionately desire what is right? What kind of knowledge do we need to gain to understand that truth? Is it something that automatically happens to us? Some of us may wish that it was automatic, but the reality is that we must put serious effort into it. Many times, we need to fight hard to overcome obstacles that get in our way. Sometimes, we may need help from our trusted friends to overcome certain kinds of challenges. We have to work hard and persevere regardless of the roadblocks we encounter.

I find that it is also important that we continually encourage ourselves even if we don't have others doing that for us. We can speak out phrases like this: "I will passionately pursue what is right" or "I will work hard at pleasing my Master." Speaking such phrases to ourselves is a powerful tool that we can use when we grow weak in our effort to overcome obstacles. Reminding ourselves of what we know to be true is a great way to keep us going in the right direction even when roadblocks present themselves in our path.

While our passion will give us the energy to continue, our pursuit of knowledge will give us the tools that we need to overcome the roadblocks. Passion and the pursuit of knowledge will bring excellence to everything we do in life. I think we should reword the quote that says, "Practice makes perfect" with a more apropos quote that could read, "Practice makes excellent." We ought to be people who practice until we get it right and never give up until we accomplish what we set out to do. When we combine passion and the pursuit of knowledge into our daily lives, we can achieve excellence. We can see excellence in what we do when we do our absolute personal best.

I am sure you have noticed that *your* personal best is different than your neighbor's personal best. That is not a bad thing by any means; it is just a different thing. Each one of us knows how much we can do when we put all our efforts into it. As you probably know, our personal best today may be better than our personal best from yesterday. That is a good thing because it means that we are improving. As we passionately pursue what is right, we keep getting better and better each day of our lives.

Ready for some homework? I want to give you a quick assessment that can help you identify your level of commitment to the principle of excellence. Give it a try and see how committed you are to the principle of excellence:

- Do I hunger and thirst for what is right?
- Does my passion for good and worthwhile cause guide my daily steps even if my friends do not encourage me?
- Do I invest time and effort into pursuing knowledge that helps me become excellent at what I do?
- Am I ready to change the world for the better by taking action and going beyond just words?

I hope you answered *yes* to each of the questions listed above. If you are not sure about your answers or need some encouragement, please find a way to get that encouragement right away. You could ask someone to encourage you with their words or you can take the time to read people's stories of perseverance. I get a lot of encouragement when I read stories like the one in the Christian scriptures of the widow whose husband passed away and who found herself in need of protection.[3] You may be familiar with the story. The woman's rights were being violated and she sought relief from a local judge. The judge had other matters to attend to and tried to ignore the woman hoping she would soon go away. However, the persistent widow was not easily dissuaded; she knew where to find the answer to her problems and passionately pursued the uncaring judge so he could provide the solution that she needed.

When Jesus told that story to his climbing companions he was encouraging and reminding them that we all ought to pray about and pursue what is right without ceasing. The widow hungered for righteousness, that is, vindication, from a judge who was unrighteous. She did her personal best day after day and did not give up. Eventually, she got what she was after when the judge could no longer ignore her passionate pursuit of what was right. We too ought to hunger for righteousness on a daily basis. That is the way of the Master.

The more we learn about the principle of excellence, the more of a responsibility we have. One of those responsibilities is to teach young people how to pursue what is right. It is easy to give up when one is young, and things appear to be overly difficult. Sadly, there are many young people who give up on life and look for ways to end it. They become overwhelmed by the many challenges they face. From the year 2006 to 2016, the suicide rate among teens ages 10 to 14 years old increased by 100%.[4] That is such a disturbing statistic! That statistic is a call to action for all of us. We, adults, must step up our involvement in the lives of young people. We need to spend time with them, mentoring them, listening to them, and giving them sound guidance by speaking truth to them. That is the only way we can change that statistic.

Other statistics about today's youth are alarming, too. The rate of depression among teens is increasing. Violence among young people is becoming more and more serious. Anxiety is very common among middle and high schoolers. All these trends ought to be a call to action for everyone. We must equip young people with the right tools so they can navigate through the challenges of life. We must find ways to stay in communication with them even though most of them would rather glue their eyes to an electronic gadget than speak with us. Telling stories like the one about the widow mentioned above or our personal stories of struggle and victory are good ways to connect with our kids.

We must also teach young people about the importance of doing their personal best. We need to help them understand that the idea is not to compare oneself to others but to compare our personal best of today with our personal best from yesterday. Teach them to look at what they are doing today and find ways to improve on what they were doing yesterday, or last week, or last year. When we teach young people that they need to put effort into doing their personal best, they will start seeing that their actions have consequences and that they have control over various aspects of their life. **Hopelessness loses its power when we know we can make things happen by our own efforts.**

We also need to teach young people how to identify their passion for making a difference in this world and help them see how to feed that passion by gaining knowledge. When we do that, we are giving them tools to overcome discouragement and some of the other negative attacks that will surely come their way throughout their life.

One of the stories that I like to read when I am facing major challenges in my own life is the life story of movie superstar Sylvester Stallone who starred as Rocky Balboa, the boxer. You probably have watched at least one of the Rocky movies, or maybe all of them. If you have not, I encourage you to get some popcorn and set time aside to watch it. Even better, sit down and watch it with young people whom you are mentoring so you can talk about it together. You probably know that Stallone's real life was not that different from the life of the boxer he played in the movie. Here is some background about Stallone's life that could make for a very interesting discussion with young people.

The real Sylvester Stallone was born in New York City in 1946. His father later moved him to Washington D.C. Young Stallone spent a good portion of his early life in foster homes because of the extremely difficult relationship that his parents had with each other. He struggled emotionally and was expelled from several schools before he finally dropped out to pursue his passion for acting and script writing.

It is interesting to me that a young man who faced so many struggles in his early life would figure out that the best way to move forward and succeed was to pursue his passion. I often wonder who may have mentored him during those teenage years and encouraged him to pursue what he was gifted in. Stallone found ways to learn everything he could about acting and script writing. His pursuit of knowledge did not pay off in the short term though.

By the 1970s, Stallone made his way back to the Big Apple after being homeless and struggling to find people who were interested in his scripts and his acting. Life in the big city continued to be difficult for Stallone and sometime in 1975 he was so broke that he ended up selling his most precious possession for $25, his dog, Butkus.

One would think that the best thing for someone like Stallone to do when things were that bad would be to get a minimum wage job and quit wasting time trying to write and act. But people who focus on always doing their personal best know that working hard at what they are passionate about will allow them to become better at it with each day that passes. **You and I ought to work today at improving what we did yesterday and tomorrow we will improve on what we did today.** Doing our personal best ought to continue day after day.

Stallone spent a lot of time and put a lot of effort into trying to sell his scripts during those difficult days. After completing his Rocky script, he decided that not only did he want to sell his script, but he also wanted to be the main character in that movie. He knocked on many doors and talked to many people until he eventually received an offer for the script. Understandably, the producers did not want Stallone to play the main role but wanted an actor with more acting experience. However, Stallone refused. The producers finally offered him a cameo appearance in the flick. Amazingly, as broke as he was, Stallone turned down various offers up to $350,000. For the following days, negotiations continued, and the producers eventually gave into Stallone's acting demands by offering him $35,000 for the movie script and letting him be the main star.

If we pursue our life calling with excellence and perseverance, we will eventually see results. A moment had arrived in Stallone's life when he could finally begin to see that his efforts were starting to pay off. He was so hopeful for his own future that he even went back to look for his dog Butkus. It took a long, difficult and confrontational negotiation with the dog's new owner before Stallone was able to get his dog back by paying the outrageous sum of $15,000 for it. The dog later made an appearance in the Academy Award-winning drama *Rocky* (1976).

Sylvester Stallone went on to become a world-renowned actor after Rocky won best picture, best directing, best film editing, and he was even nominated for best actor. Other scripts and movies followed. A paralyzed lip and slurred speech did not hold him back from becoming a superstar. Posters and toy figures of Stallone as Rocky or Rambo became popular and we can even find some of them today. Sylvester Stallone's life story reminds us that true success in life requires doing our personal best with perseverance and we do it regardless of how many obstacles end up in our path.

When we observe how people of excellence do what they do, we end up discovering that they do what most other people are not willing to do. But what is it that they do differently? Author Sam Parker found a way to clearly explain this one thing that people of excellence do. In his book *212: The Extra Degree*, Parker explains that, "At 211 degrees, water is hot. At 212 degrees, it boils. And with boiling water, comes steam. And with steam, you can power a train. Just one extra degree makes all the difference."[5] People of excellence go up by one extra degree. They do whatever it takes to get to where they know they need to be and then they consistently put in one extra degree of work.

In his book *Making it Happen*, author Charles Paul Conn encourages us to put in one extra degree of work in our ministry efforts. Conn calls it stretching ourselves, "Whatever it is, however impossible it seems, if it is noble, if it is consistent with God's kingdom, you must hunger after it and stretch yourself to reach it."[6]

I hope I have been able to encourage you to give that extra degree of work to your God-given purpose and mission and to stretch yourself to reach it. I also hope that you will continue pursuing knowledge to become the best version of yourself. There is literally no limit to how much you and I can accomplish if we follow our passion, gain knowledge, and choose to live a life of excellence.

* * *

TAKE AWAY: We work today at improving on what we did yesterday and tomorrow we will improve on what we did today.

GIVE AWAY: Keep striving for the best and do not settle for what is average.

9

Compassion

Blessed are the merciful, for they will be shown mercy.[1]

It was the last leg of our trip and the airplane touched down at Netaji Subhas Chandra Bose International Airport in Calcutta, India. I was filled with great but nervous anticipation. Months before, I had written a letter to Mother Teresa of Calcutta and she responded to me in her own handwriting. It is interesting to me that a letter can say so much about a person by the way it is written. Mother Teresa's letter was simple, yet she spoke through it with authority about how and when I could come to visit her work. She spoke of her humble ministry home but invited me with open arms. I had read that letter many times before that day when we landed in Calcutta.

Nothing can really prepare you for what you are about to encounter when you get to Calcutta. The city challenges all your senses from the very moment you arrive. The streets are crowded, the cars and people intermingle on the roads, the smells and pollution challenge your lungs, temperatures vary throughout the year with monsoon season being the most difficult, poverty and sickness surround you, and there is no doubt whatsoever that you are in a place of great human need.

Early the next morning, we got up and got ready to venture into the chaos and sensory overload that is Calcutta. I had taken a group of college students with me on this trip so they could experience serving in a place of great need. We made our way to Mother Teresa's home for the dying. The very name of the place helped us begin our mental preparation for what we were about to experience. Mother Teresa's Roman Catholic Order of the Missionaries of Charity is a congregation of women dedicated to the poor and destitute of India and other places around the world. The Sisters from this congregation manage all aspects of the home for the dying.

When we arrived, we had a short welcome followed by clear instructions on the work we could do that day. We quickly learned that the Sisters spend little time talking and most of their time laboring to meet the needs of the many people who frequently arrive at the home seeking help. The Sister who received us explained that every one of the residents of this home would soon die and that our job was to do our best so they could die with dignity.

Within a short time of being there, we all had brushes, brooms, soap, and cleaning rags in our hands along with specific assignments on how to serve. As we received our assignments, one of our college students, Karen, leaned over and said in a quiet voice to me, "Lori, I don't touch filth. Please know that."

I responded to her, "Karen, look around you in this city; you are breathing filth."

The Sister who was handing out the assignments interrupted us and said in her Indian accent to Karen, "Take this soap and bucket. Go to that lady there and clean her. She has made a mess and needs a new diaper. After you clean her and bathe her, put this clean dress on her."

Karen and I were speechless; neither she nor I had ever cared for another person like that. Without any delay, the Sister took me to my assignment, and we left Karen standing there and looking at me in disbelief. We all went about doing our assigned duties for the day.

Prior to our departure from the U.S., we had done a trip orientation for the group. At that orientation, I had encouraged every one of the college students to apply the Gospel of Jesus to everyone they would meet during the trip.

At the guest house that evening, Karen told us that she had found herself not knowing how to apply the Gospel of Jesus to a dying Indian lady. As we talked, Karen soon realized that she had actually started living out the Gospel of Jesus the moment she picked up that piece of soap.

I encouraged Karen to share her impressions of our first service day with the rest of the group. She said, "I wasn't sure what I was going to do when I was asked to clean that lady's mess... She weighed 60 pounds at best... Doing the best I could, I took off her filthy dress and diaper... I cleaned her and I bathed her... Then, I put a new diaper and a clean dress on her..."

Karen was having a hard time describing the experience and I could tell something was different with her. She told us that one of the Sisters had explained to her that the Indian lady had previously become a Christian. Karen also told us that the little lady did not speak English but that knowing she was a Christian had, in a different kind of way, made it easier to communicate with her.

Karen continued recounting for us what had taken place that morning, "What do you do with someone who is so helpless? I didn't know what to do after I bathed her... So, I picked her up, cradle her in my arms, and rocked her back and forth. I felt that I needed to sing to her, so I started singing,

> *'Jesus loves me this I know for the Bible tells me so, little ones to him belong, they are weak, but he is strong. Yes, little-Indian lady, Jesus loves you. Yes, little-Indian lady, Jesus loves you. Yes, little-Indian lady, Jesus ...'*

"I looked down and she had left this world while I was singing and holding her in my arms."

We all got quiet and still as Karen finished sharing. That Indian lady, who was a climbing companion of Jesus, had left this world while hearing and feeling the love of her compassionate new friend who had come to be with her from across the world. Our own personal experiences from that day along with Karen's sharing that night had taught us that we cannot truly show compassion until we get past our five senses. We realized that we can allow neither smells nor tastes nor sights nor feelings nor sounds to keep us from helping the needy in this world; we ought to show love in action to them. That is compassion at its best.

We also learned that it does not matter where we come from, what language we speak, the color our skin is, or what our past looks like; what does matter when we find ourselves face-to-face with human need is that we respond, right there and then, with compassion. There is no need to go someplace for a while and think about it before we respond—we must take a moment to understand the need and then immediately respond to it.

Jesus told his climbing companions on that mountainside long ago, "Blessed are the merciful, for they will be shown mercy."[2] Many of us have heard Newton's third law of motion that states that for every action, there is an equal and opposite reaction. Jesus was telling his climbing companions on that day that the principle of compassion works just like that. **We must show compassion to others so that we can receive the blessing of compassion ourselves; there is action and an equal reaction.**

At our non-profit organization, we equip caring adults as mentors so that they can teach young people about universal principles, and one of those principles is the principle of compassion. We define compassion as love in action, caring for others, and having sympathy for another person's suffering. Compassion is lived out when we allow *understanding* and *responsiveness* to guide our behavior.

Understanding occurs when we allow ourselves to be sympathetic to someone's hurt and become aware of other people's feelings. Responsiveness takes place when we respond by acting to help someone in need. Our friend, Karen, did exactly that at the home for the dying. She allowed herself to understand the real need of that frail Indian lady and responded by doing something about it. Her need was more than just being bathed; it also was to experience love as she was living her last few moments of life on this earth.

Sometimes, we choose to substitute compassion with pity. Pity is the *feeling* of sorrow and compassion. The *feeling* of pity, in and of itself, is not a bad thing but it must lead us to show compassion. Pity should guide us to understand the human need set before us and then lead us to immediately respond. All too often, the feeling of pity, unfortunately, gives many of us the mistaken idea that we have done our work. We think that just because we felt pity our job is done and we can keep moving on. People who live by the principle of compassion have learned to use the feeling of pity to propel them forward to show compassion instead of just walking by.

The Messiah told his climbing companions that there will be a moment at the end of this earth, and the beginning of the new one, when he would acknowledge his true climbing companions because they took care of the hungry, the sick, and the destitute.[3] This is the best motivation to be people of compassion. We do not need to anxiously look for the limelight here on earth when we know we will have much better limelight and reward at the end of time. He said it! He said he will choose us as his own. Surely you are as excited about this announcement as I am!

My mom would always tell us, kids, "Kill them with kindness." Back then, I thought it was an odd request coming from my mom. I would question in my head how I could actually kill someone with kindness. But, as the years went by, I began to fully understand the wisdom contained within my mom's saying. I now understand that it meant that I am *not* to stop showing kindness to everyone while I still have breath.

We can read about the earlier years of the Jewish people and their many celebrations in the Older Testament. One of those celebrations was the Year of Jubilee.[4] All debts were forgiven in that specified year, which occurred every 50 years. The Jewish people had it in their calendar, and it was a time when all things could start anew. The priests and overseers instructed all Jewish citizens not to hold grudges on that year. Slaves were set free. Bondage was broken so people could start over. It was the ultimate time of respite so that people could rest from their labor and hard work. The Year of Jubilee was facilitated restoration in the land. I think that this was such a great idea because it was also time to demonstrate compassion toward everyone. What a great thing for Jewish citizens to be reminded that everyone was to understand everyone else's needs and respond to those needs.

We, climbing companions, do not need to wait 50 years before we show compassion to others. We need to allow compassion to freely flow from us as we go about our daily routines. We can have a Day of Jubilee, instead of a Year of Jubilee, every day of our lives. From personal experience, I know that for compassion to freely flow from us we must first self-reflect. I encourage you to ask yourself some questions that I have found very useful in my journey to become a compassionate person. You can also add your own questions to this list:

- Will I choose to do something about injustice or sit idly instead?
- Will I show up to volunteer when I see a need?
- Will I send clothes to those who don't have them?
- Will I give money to those who are lacking?
- Will I take action or just keep on walking by?
- Will I ...?

Not long ago, José and I were working with our team in the beautiful city of Cape Town, South Africa. Our team, led by our National Director, Dominique, goes into the public schools to mentor kids in some of the most challenging neighborhoods. Some of those schools are dangerous but our staff and volunteer mentors persevere and do not give up for the sake of those kids. Slowly but surely, kids' lives are changing for the better as a result of their work.

One morning, while it was still dark, we got up early to go for a run before we met Dominique for breakfast. We made our way down some streets and, as usual, José led us into neighborhoods we did not know. He cannot seem to stay on the main streets but always wants to go deep into the culture wherever we are visiting. As we ran, we passed an open dirt field between some houses and noticed what looked like a person lying in the middle of the field. We slowly approached that spot and saw an older lady lying there. José called out to her and touched her shoulder but there was no response.

Suddenly, we heard a voice approaching us from behind. It was a man's voice, but we could not understand what he had just said. We waited for him to come to where we were standing. He was a short older man, his skin was dark and wrinkled, he was dressed in old worn-out clothes, and it was obvious that his hair had not been combed in quite a while. He smiled with a toothless smile and said now in heavily accented English, "I tell her not to drink but she doesn't listen. Other people give her alcohol and she drinks it when I'm not watching." He squatted next to her and tried to help her sit up. She said something, in what sounded like Xhosa (one of the South African languages) to us and fought to lie down again. The older man continued smiling at us and talking with her in Xhosa.

We found ourselves not knowing what to do at that moment. We looked at each other as if to say, these people are drunks and we just need to keep on walking by. However, neither one of us chose to walk away. So, we asked him, "What is your name?"

He replied in English, "My name is David and she is Antie[5] Marie."

We asked, "Is there something we can do for you?"

He replied, "We are fine. I just need to get her up and away from this field. I just need to take her there under those trees where I'm trying to build a fire."

I wasn't sure I wanted to go under those trees, but we asked him again, "What else can we help you with? Do you need food?"

He said, "Food is good."

We didn't have anything with us so we said, "We can buy some food. What kind of food do you want? Bread and water?"

"Bread is good. We don't need water. Coffee is good, too—the men like coffee. Any dry food will be good."

José and I waved goodbye and left. We were wondering if it made sense to come back but we had promised David some food. We quickly returned to the hotel, cleaned up, and drove our rental car to the nearest grocery store. We bought several food items including some coffee grounds. David's request for coffee seemed odd to me. He had said the *men* liked coffee. Was I confused by his accent or did he really say, "the men liked coffee"?

We drove back to the dirt field, walked to the trees, and found the two of them. Antie Marie was sitting up and David was messing with a little fire. When he saw us, David smiled his toothless smile. He got up and was visibly happy. We gave him the groceries. We knew we needed to get going quickly because of our meeting with Dominique. We asked David if we could pray for the two of them. He smiled and agreed.

We laid hands on the two of them and prayed for God to bless them and provide for them in the name of our Lord Jesus Christ. We finished our prayer and looked at David. He had his hands raised and was looking up to the heavens. We silently asked ourselves, "Does David know who the Lord Jesus Christ is?" Our time was limited so we said goodbye and got back into our car.

Neither one of us could stop thinking about David throughout that day. Something was different about him, but we could not figure out what. We decided to go back to that same dirt field the next morning during our workout time. We were not sure why we needed to go back but something kept pulling on us to go see David again.

We got to the same spot but there were no signs of David. We found ourselves intensely looking for him. We looked in the woods but found nothing. There was a little drizzle that morning and we wondered how David and Antie Marie could stay dry and stay warm. We continued walking down the street. A couple of blocks away, we spotted David walking in front of a store. We hurried there to see what he was doing.

We got to the small building and found David walking among eight bodies that were lying down side by side under a little roof that stretched out from the building. He was covering one of the guys with an old blanket and propping another guy up with some rags that he used as a pillow. The scene was surreal. As we were standing on the porch looking at David do his work, a man that we assumed to be the store owner stuck his head out from inside the store and told us they were closed for another couple of hours.

We were still trying to understand what we were seeing so we pointed at David and said to the man at the door that we were just looking for him to see if he needed something. The store owner said, "Oh, him. Yes, he is a good bloke. I let him bring his friends and sleep under this little roof until I open the store. It's the least I can do. He is always taking care of all his boets [friends]. Totsiens [goodbye]." With that, he went back inside.

At that moment we realized what we had been feeling all along. This toothless, dark skin, wrinkled face, beautiful older man was no ordinary man. This man was one of the best examples of a godly and compassionate man that either of us had ever seen. He was homeless but had made his life purpose taking care of the homeless. He was trying to keep Antie Marie from getting drunk, he was getting food and coffee for the men, he had found a shelter to get them out of the rain, and he was offering them love with words and action.

David is today, I'm sure wherever he is, giving everything that he has to others. We remember him from time to time and pray for him. But we are thankful that God let us get a glimpse of what compassion looks like by bringing us in contact with David. **May we become so committed to meet other people's needs that we are willing to offer love in action each day of our lives.**

An early Christian leader by the name of James wrote one of the first letters that we find in the newer testament of the Christian scriptures. Many historians believe that James was the oldest of Jesus' brothers. We know that James originally misunderstood and challenged Jesus and his ministry but eventually came to realize that his brother was the real Messiah. James went on to become the leader of the early church.

Many believe that James wrote his letter to Christian Jews who had fled Jerusalem because of persecution. James explains to the recipients of his letter that the Lord is coming full of mercy and compassion for those who endure hardship.[6] He also very clearly challenged those early Christians to demonstrate their faith with their actions. James explained to them that only those followers of Jesus who practice love in action are true to their faith.[7] Those words ought to resonate loudly with us today just as they likely did to those Christian Jews. We must practice love in action, not just words, in order to be true to our faith.

If you have read the poem titled "Judge Softly," you will probably agree with me that is a great treasure. It was penned by community activist Mary T. Lathrap in 1895. The wisdom contained within just a few stanzas of this poem is one of the best teachings we can find on the principle of compassion. I think we should try to read it to our children and help them become acquainted with it. Some people have extracted a quote out of this poem which others have incorrectly credited as a Native

American proverb. Nevertheless, the quote serves as a powerful reminder of how we, climbing companions of Jesus, ought to think about those people whom we meet and who are in need.

A common version of the quote is, "Don't pass judgment on another person until you have walked a mile in their moccasins." Children reading this for the first time may ask, "What does walking a mile in someone else's moccasins have to do with being merciful or showing compassion?" That is a great question and it gives us an opportunity to explain a very important concept. We cannot fully understand someone's motivation, sorrows, wounds, or joys until we have experienced those same things ourselves. In other words, we must first walk in their moccasins. Because of this, it is best for us not to pass judgment on others when we encounter human need.

I know that many times, it seems much easier to judge someone for the situation in which they find themselves than for us to take time to help them. But rather than passing judgment, it is best if we try to see ourselves in their situation. We can more accurately decide what our response ought to be to a person in need when we take time to walk in his or her moccasins. We need to either walk in that person's moccasins or do our best to picture ourselves in them before we can show love to them. This is what compassionate people do; they envision or put themselves in other people's situations so they can somehow feel some of what they feel. That is the way of the Master. He put himself in our situation so he could show us the right way.

I decided to include Mary Lathrap's poem here. I encourage you to set time aside to read and meditate on it. I also hope you find time to share this poem and what it means with your own children or those whom you may have an opportunity to mentor. May you and I respond promptly to other people's needs and judge them softly each day of our lives.

Pray, don't find fault with the man that limps,
Or stumbles along the road.
Unless you have worn the moccasins he wears,
Or stumbled beneath the same load.
There may be tears in his soles that hurt
Though hidden away from view.
The burden he bears placed on your back
May cause you to stumble and fall, too.
Don't sneer at the man who is down today
Unless you have felt the same blow
That caused his fall or felt the shame
That only the fallen know.
You may be strong, but still the blows
That were his, unknown to you in the same way,
May cause you to stagger and fall, too.
Don't be too harsh with the man that sins.
Or pelt him with words, or stone, or disdain.
Unless you are sure you have no sins of your own,
And it's only wisdom and love that your heart contains.
For you know if the tempter's voice
Should whisper as soft to you,
As it did to him when he went astray,
It might cause you to falter, too.
Just walk a mile in his moccasins
Before you abuse, criticize and accuse.
If just for one hour, you could find a way
To see through his eyes, instead of your own muse.
I believe you'd be surprised to see
That you've been blind and narrow minded, even unkind.

There are people on reservations and in the ghettos
Who have so little hope, and too much worry on their
minds.
Brother, there but for the grace of God go you and I.
Just for a moment, slip into his mind and traditions
And see the world through his spirit and eyes
Before you cast a stone or falsely judge his conditions.
Remember to walk a mile in his moccasins
And remember the lessons of humanity taught to you by
your elders.
We will be known forever by the tracks we leave
In other people's lives, our kindnesses and generosity.
Take the time to walk a mile in his moccasins.[8]

* * *

TAKE AWAY: If you don't get beyond the five senses, you will struggle to show true compassion.

GIVE AWAY: Walk a mile in another person's moccasins.

10

Humility

"You're blessed when you're at the end of your rope. With less of you there is more of God and his rule. You're blessed when you feel you've lost what is most dear to you. Only then can you be embraced by the One most dear to you."[1]

Ordinarily, we go to church with a cheerful attitude as we anticipate worshiping God with friends. But on this day, our family drove to church in silence as we all felt an overwhelming downcast spirit within us. For José and me, this was by far the most difficult day we had experienced together as a family. On that day, we were holding a celebration of life service for our son, Colin Andrew.

There is no true emotional preparation that one can do for a day like this. One goes through the motions and hopes to be able to say and do what is needed at the appropriate time and to the appropriate people.

When we arrived at the church, we met with our pastor and went over an outline for the service. Our pastor said it would be nice if we had an open microphone at the end of the service in case someone wanted to say a few words about Colin. We agreed.

As the service unfolded, it was truly a celebration of life. Lyndsee, Colin's girlfriend, had prepared a very nice collection of pictures on the big screen and music that all of us enjoyed. Our son, Kenan, spoke about carrying on with Colin's passion to change the world with his work. Our worship pastor did a great job encouraging us through music. We approached the end of the service and our pastor announced that anyone who wanted to speak a few words about Colin could do so at that time.

Our friend, Barry, stood up and did a great job recalling many events in Colin's 22 years of life here on earth. Then, another person walked up to the microphone and shared about Colin's impact on his life. Then, a middle-aged lady, whom we didn't know, walked up to the microphone and spoke about Colin ministering and helping her make a significant change in her life. Then, came a young man who shared about Colin's influence in his life. Pretty soon, a line formed in front of the microphone. Each of them told one story after another about Colin's love for others, dedication to helping others, commitment to Christ, humble service when someone was in need, and so much more.

We did not realize it at the time but the service lasted more than three hours. The church was full of people wanting to *honor* our 22-year young son. The pastor allowed everyone who wanted to share about Colin's life to have a chance to do so. Everyone in our family was overwhelmed with joy as we heard every one of those people share about the difference Colin had made in their lives. We knew he was a great young man and that he was committed to his faith, but we had no idea of the magnitude and far-reaching effect of his love and commitment to others.

What will people say at our own celebration of life service? There is a verse in the Newer Testament of the Christian scriptures that describes what we experienced that day during Colin's celebration of life. "So humble yourselves under the mighty power of God, and at the right time he will lift you up in honor."[2] As I read this verse, I came to realize that those words were a description of something that took place in Colin's life and that can take place in any of our lives also. The words in this verse are a promise that one of Jesus' first climbing companions, Peter, decided to share with people of his day. We also have the blessing of being able to read them.

Colin had humbled himself in the way he lived his life and he was truly lifted that day. He was lifted into eternity as he was lifted in honor. Colin's life journey was not easy. He did the common things that most people do. He went to school and graduated from college. He did crazy things and got into trouble as most kids and teens do. But he always came around to make things right with God. He spent his last couple of years on this earth serving people in the rain forest of Costa Rica.

In the prime of his life, Colin contracted an infection that spread through his bloodstream within days. On April 9, José received the kind of phone call that no one ever wants to receive. That was the day when Colin unexpectedly went to heaven. Even his departure from this world and into the next was done with little to no fanfare. Colin had a way to humbly do everything he did. I am thankful for the many memories José and I have of him and for the tremendous positive influence he had on each of our lives.

Colin had heartfelt conversations with just about anyone he met. He often spoke to José about the hard work and effort that it took to transform one's mind and detach from what the world had to offer. But over time, Colin came to understand, through much studying and intentional living, what it meant to live a godly life. We miss Colin's physical presence daily. José and I found a beautiful spot under a tree that we have dedicated to Colin as a place where we go and talk about the influence, he still has on people today. Colin is in heaven now, but we enjoy reminiscing about the way he lived his life as a living sacrifice before his unexpected physical departure.

The Newer Testament urges us to be *living sacrifices*. "Therefore, I urge you, brothers and sisters, in view of God's mercy, to offer your bodies as a living sacrifice, holy and pleasing to God—this is your true and proper worship."[3] One may ask, "What is a living sacrifice?" When we become climbing companions of Jesus, we are called to live our lives as *living sacrifices*. It is perhaps better for us to ask ourselves: How can I live in such a way that my life is a living sacrifice? I think we should put this question up on billboards next to our interstates and create social media campaigns with it so everyone in the world can be reminded. Well, I may be expecting too much. It's just that I know that not many people walk around saying, "I am so glad that my life is a living sacrifice." I also know that it is not a popular life goal or a highly rated New Year resolution in our world today although I wish that it was.

It is probably best if we start by understanding what a sacrifice is. A sacrifice is that one thing that we consecrate (set apart) and offer to God. Jesus Christ gave us the best example ever of how to present his body as a living sacrifice. He dedicated his life to a divine purpose; he sacrificed his life by consecrating and offering it to God. I know most of us will never be asked to give our lives in the same way as the Messiah did, but we should still get ready as if someday we would be asked to do so. **Our first step ought to be to consciously make the choice to live a godly life.**

For all of us, there comes the time when we must decide whether we want to live a worldly life or a godly life. We really don't have a choice in the matter, we must decide one way or the other as to the kind of life we will live. If we don't consciously decide, we will end up living a worldly life, by default.

A couple of thousand years ago, an unknown author wrote a letter to a very confused group of people and encouraged them to get it together and start living their lives right. Though not identified specifically in the letter, it is understood by style in vocabulary that the author was the apostle John, one of Jesus' early climbing companions. In the letter, John described the world as having three main characteristics that can keep us from being living sacrifices. These characteristics are the desires of the flesh, the desires of the eyes, and the pride of life.[4]

I like the clarity of that teaching because it was very helpful to me when I was old enough to understand that I needed to decide on how I wanted to live my life.

Climbing companions strive to be humble and live their lives by continuously consecrating their flesh, eyes, and self-esteem. It is not easy to do because the world is constantly pushing us in the opposite direction. But, we must do it. We ought to present our bodies as living sacrifices. In no priority order, we need to consecrate our flesh by asking God to help us master and control the excessive physical desires for food, drink, sex, stimulants, etc. We need to consecrate our eyes by asking God to help us master and control the envy we may have when we see all the great and beautiful things others have. We need to consecrate our self-esteem by asking God to help us master and control the ambitions that puff us up and make us feel that we are above others.

When we commit to doing that on an ongoing basis, we begin to live by the principle of humility. Humble people don't walk around telling others about their humility because humility is the recognition and use of our strengths and abilities for the purpose of benefiting others without us seeking any credit or reward. Humility is thinking more of others than ourselves and not demanding praise for our good works. Humility is also the opposite of conceit. Conceit is thinking of oneself more than others, excessive pride in oneself, vanity, and self-admiration. There is no room for any of those traits in the life of a climbing companion of Jesus.

I remember my father, Gerald Marvel, telling me with great emphasis that the *towel* was the symbol of humility. Dad came to the graduation ceremony when I received my doctorate degree and told me he was proud of my educational achievement. He also wanted to make sure that I understood that earning that degree and having a *title* also meant earning a responsibility. As we were still on the university campus after the ceremony, he said to me, **"it is not about the *title*, it's about the *towel*."** He explained to me that the towel he was referring to was the towel that Jesus the Messiah used to dry the feet of his climbing companions hours before his death.[5] He said to me with clear delivery, "It is about being a servant."

I agree with my dad that it is indeed about the *towel*. Many today talk about servant leadership but I prefer to stay away from that title. I stay away from it because the emphasis is often on leadership, not on service. I think what great leaders do best is *humble servanthood*. **When we serve with humility, we most certainly lead people. What a noble responsibility!**

Humility is what happens when *healthy self-esteem* and *servant-hood* intersect. When that intersection happens in our daily contact with others, it is not only about serving others, it is about knowing who we are while we serve. In other words, it is about our heart condition when we serve. That is why I am convinced beyond any doubt that a leader must be a person who lives by the principle of humility in order to effectively lead. Climbing companions of Jesus ought to be leaders of humility because that is the way he led and expects us to lead—that is the way of the Master.

The Messiah taught that those who are humble enough to recognize that they are spiritually helpless, in poverty, and accept who they are will be comforted at the right time and in the right way. He said, "Blessed are the poor in spirit, for theirs is the kingdom of heaven. Blessed are those who mourn, for they will be comforted."[6] Jesus wanted his climbing companions to recognize their spiritual poverty, develop a heart of acceptance, and be of service to others.

Christian scriptures present us with many teachings about how we ought to see ourselves. They do not say we ought to think of ourselves as superior or lower than everyone else. They clearly and simply say we ought to think of ourselves with clear-minded and serious judgment.[7] To think too lowly or too highly of oneself is simply bad theology.

I meet many people who see themselves so very low and continuously compare themselves to others. I try to encourage them, but some seem to have a hard time stopping that kind of thinking. We, climbing companions, are not to see ourselves that way. If we think and act that way, that makes us disobedient to the teachings of Jesus. He wants us to see ourselves as children of God.

On the other hand, far too many people in our society see themselves as being superior to others. This kind of thinking is also disobedient to what the Christian scriptures teach us and can be poisonous to others. It is the root cause of much evil in our society such as racism, gender inequality, age discrimination, lack of respect towards others, and more.

We, climbing companions, must think of ourselves with sober judgment; we must think of ourselves *just right*. It is like cooking spaghetti; it needs to be done just right—*al dente*. I love spaghetti (not the calories) but I don't enjoy it when it is poorly cooked. You can either undercook spaghetti or overcook it and neither one is good. It is such a pleasure when it is cooked just right though. A person with self-esteem that is healthy is a person who thinks of herself or himself just right. What a pleasure it is to do life with those people.

I know that we sometimes may feel low about something that happened but that is different than thinking lowly of ourselves. If I ever feel down about something that I did because it did not turn out just the way I thought it should, I like to read the book of Psalms. I especially like to read Psalm 139:13-16 (NIV):

> *"For you created my inmost being; I praise you because I am fearfully and wonderfully made; your works are wonderful, I know that full well. My frame was not hidden from you when I was made in the secret place. When I was woven together in the depths of the earth, your eyes saw my unformed body. All the days ordained for me were written in your book before one of them came to be."[8]*

I mentioned this because challenges do abound in all of our lives and daily situations present us with decisions, we must make that can make us feel either high or low. Think about what you would do if you were the leader of a very prosperous and thriving organization and all of the sudden, without much warning, all of your employees left you and went to work for a new startup business in town. Even if you liked the founder of the new startup, how would you react to your employees leaving your company? Well, that is exactly what happened to the last prophet whose life is recorded in the Christian scriptures.

Jesus Christ came in the flesh to this earth and came to the very same location where John the Baptizer was doing great ministry work. Rather than getting angry or resentful about his followers leaving him, John responded with humility and encouraged his followers to follow their new teacher. John even went as far as to say, "I must become less."[9] He told his followers, "No one can receive anything unless God gives it from heaven."[10] John had a clear view of himself. He knew who he was and what his work was all about, but he also was quick to recognize that it was time for him to encourage every one of his followers to follow their new leader—Jesus.

Our self-esteem is badly affected when we start comparing ourselves to others. Nothing good can come out of that exercise. I know that on any given day, there are many people out there who have more talents and successes than I do. If I allow that to become my focus and compare myself to them, I will end up going crazy. Or worse, I will become a vindictive person. It is simply not a healthy thing for me to do. My self-esteem can only get healthier when I focus on my talents and gifts and when I do the best I can with what I have been given from above. Please know that if we do not have confidence in ourselves, we will be limited in how we comfort, love or serve others. When we have a biblical and healthy self-esteem, we can serve others more effectively.

The Latin phrase *Imago Dei* is a perfect reminder of who we were created to be. To me, this phrase contains a promise, an assurance, a purpose, and a responsibility all packed into one holism. When that phrase is translated, it means "the image of

God." In an unpublished paper, Fuller Theological Seminary professor Bruce Ware wrote, "The image of God in man as functional holism means that God made human beings, both male and female, to be created and finite representations (images of God) of God's own nature, that in relationship with him and each other, they might be his representatives (imaging God) in carrying out the responsibilities he has given to them."[11]

Imago Dei is a holism that tells us we can have the assurance that we are not random cosmic creations but instead intricately created beings who bear the image of God. Not only that but we were also created with a purpose to do certain significant things here on earth that God himself decided in advance to assign to us. That means we have the privilege of carrying out divinely ordained responsibilities. Wow! The apostle Paul realized that we needed to know this. He penned this reminder in a letter addressed to people whom he had probably never met. Paul said, "we are God's handiwork, created in Christ Jesus to do good works, which God prepared in advance for us to do."[12]

When we have a clear view of ourselves, we can more effectively carry out the responsibilities assigned to us by God. We live out the principle of humility by how we serve while here on this earth. Servanthood is using our strengths to help others, without desperately or quietly looking for credit or expecting anything in return. People who choose to be humble grow in this choice by thinking of others most of the time. It is this others-oriented stance that can give us the opportunity to serve people with a sincere heart without ever wanting any credit for it.

When I engage in conversations about the principle of humility, there is a scene from my teenage years that immediately crosses my mind. I remember being at a convention and getting up early in the morning to pray. I was sitting on the lawn when I heard noises made by an older man as he bent over time and time again picking up something from the ground. He eventually got close enough to me and said, "Good morning." I immediately recognized who it was. It was Reverend Ben Reid, the keynote speaker at the convention. I curiously asked him what he was doing, and he simply said, "I am picking up trash." He wished me a great day, turned around and continued his cleaning project.

Here was the convention's keynote speaker picking up trash before most people woke up and went to breakfast. The man who spoke before thousands of people was cleaning up the grounds! What an example of humility! This humble man was doing something that nobody expected him to do. Furthermore, he was doing it when most people were sleeping. Reverend Ben Reid mentored me more in that single encounter than what I could have learned by reading a whole book on humility during my teenage years.

You and I can be a *Ben Reid* to young people around us. Sometimes it does not take much to encourage a young person along the right path. Other times it takes much more intentional mentoring to help them see the difference between the right and the wrong path set before them. Mentoring children and teens is an act of service that we ought to include in our lives. No one is born a good mentor, but we all could mentor others if we choose to do so. Our words and actions combined with a little bit of listening are what it takes to mentor a child. I encourage you to try it.

Serving others without receiving any credit is a great way for all of us to get started down the path of humility. Do it without fanfare or without getting noticed if possible. Just like when you help neighbors do yard work, serve at a local shelter, volunteer at the church in the nursery, or mentor kids in the schools. We need to serve in areas that either suit our gifts and talents or simply serve in areas that do not require any special talents. We all need to practice serving until it becomes a natural behavior in our life routines.

If your acts of service *do* get noticed just keep in mind that you are doing them for God and that your main goal is to please him by being obedient. However, if recognition is given to you, accept it gracefully. A simple *thank you* is enough and then you can mentally give that recognition up to God. Notice that when you say *thank you,* there is no *me* in that phrase. Some people make a big deal when someone recognizes them for their acts of service and respond with words like, "It's not *me*, it's God and not *me*, don't thank *me*." By the time they get done with their rebuttal, they have talked about "me me me" so much more than what the other person ever expected to hear. A simple *thank you* is a much humbler way to receive an affirmation. If necessary, you can say something like, "That is nice of you to say, thank you."

I believe God wants us to feel the joy of doing something well. Humility is an act of selflessness and that pleases him. Once we are equipped with the knowledge that we were created in the image of God and we have suited ourselves with the desire to help others without wanting any credit for it, we can fulfill the call that Jesus places on us, his climbing companions, to be people of humility. May you receive infinite joy as you humbly serve others.

* * *

TAKE AWAY: We are intricately created beings who bear the image of God.

GIVE AWAY: Leading others is not about the title, it's about the towel.

11

Teamwork

"You're blessed when you can show people how to cooperate instead of compete or fight. That's when you discover who you really are, and your place in God's family."[1]

I drove away from Hartsfield-Jackson Atlanta International Airport with a downtrodden spirit and a whole lot of concern. I knew this was neither the first nor likely the last time that I would drive away from that airport since my ministry work requires that I frequently fly to and from many places. But I was not doing well that afternoon. I avoided the interstates and drove home using back roads with as little traffic as possible. I did not have the emotional strength to drive in the middle of the thousands of cars that routinely fill the interstates that crisscross Atlanta. This should have been a routine drive for me but, on that day, it was not.

I had just said goodbye to my best friend, my husband, and I was feeling awful. At the airport, I had come up with many things to do as if I could slow time down. I even asked him to wait a little longer so I could take a picture of him. Eventually, I had realized that I could not delay him any longer and had kissed him goodbye. He had been patient with me by letting me slow down his departure as long as possible. As I drove home, I wonder when I would be able to talk with him again.

José had decided to go and visit his parents for Easter. He knew they were having a difficult time and was going to see what kind of help he could provide to them. Ordinarily, a trip out of the country for a few days would be fine but this trip was anything but ordinary. This trek would take him first to Colombia and then to Venezuela. Reading the news about Venezuela did not offer any encouragement to me. When he decided he would go, I checked the U.S. State Department's website and was overwhelmed by what I read:

"Reconsider travel to Venezuela due to crime, civil unrest, poor health infrastructure, and arbitrary arrest and detention of U.S. citizens. Some areas have increased risk... Do not travel... within 50 miles of the Colombian border due to crime. Violent crime, such as homicide, armed robbery, kidnapping, and carjacking, is common."[2]

I knew it made a lot of sense for him to go and see his parents, but Venezuela's situation frightened me, to say the least. In reality, I was wishing there would be another option instead of him traveling there. On that day, I drove away from the airport praying for him and wishing for time to speed up quickly until his return. Our family stateside, staff at work, and close friends joined me in prayer over José and his family. It gave me strength to know that so many people were supporting us in prayer. Our good friend, Heidi, even made it possible for José to take a satellite phone with him on his trip. Knowing that I had a way to communicate with him also gave me a little bit of encouragement during such a difficult situation.

Before the trip, José and I had spent a lot of time talking about his family's situation in Venezuela. We also had conversations about how things had gotten so bad. This country has the largest oil reserves in the world but children there are dying because they lack food and medicine. How can that be possible or even make sense?

The words spoken by Jesus on Mt. Eremos long ago answered that question for me.[3] Jesus said, "You're blessed when you can show people how to cooperate instead of compete or fight. That's when you discover who you really are, and your place in God's family."[4] Government officials in Venezuela had done nothing to cooperate with the people in their country but rather fought to gain wealth at the expense of everyone else. The result was complete chaos and misery for everyone other than themselves.

During our conversations about the situation in Venezuela, José and I wanted to believe that their high-ranking government officials would turn from their evil ways for the sake of the people who were suffering. But day after day, the facts spoke for themselves. Their government officials promoted evil by encouraging violence instead of cooperation among everyone. They had placed guns in the hands of questionable characters throughout their country to serve as a makeshift security force. Sadly, their actions demonstrated the opposite of what Jesus taught and what the Christian scriptures encourage us to do. Lawlessness was being reported every day.

When Jesus taught his climbing companions on Mt. Eremos about finding their place in God's family, he was talking about living at peace with everyone. He was explaining to them that we discover our place in God's family when we live by the principle of Teamwork. Living at peace with everyone requires *cooperation* and *effective communication*. That was not only true for Jesus' climbing companions in the culture of that day, but it was also meant to be true for any other culture anytime in history.

Time and time again, we have seen how societies collapse when their members are not peacemakers and choose not to live by the principle of teamwork. Most of us remember what we learned in history books or saw first hand in the news such as the collapse of the Roman empire, the horrific effects of the Holocaust, the breakdown of the Soviet Union, and the end of apartheid.

As José left for Venezuela, I knew he was heading into a country where its citizens have no choice but to fight in order to have most of their daily needs met. In that country, the principle of teamwork is nothing but a distant memory. In 2018, the country was listed as having one of the top three highest per capita murder rates in the world.[5] The most realistic data on murders in that country is provided by Venezuela's Violence Observatory. It placed Venezuela at 89 homicides per 100,000 of population in 2017, making that nation the most dangerous in Latin America, in a region which already has the highest homicides rates in the world. Armed civilian groups called "colectivos" initially sponsored by the Venezuelan government enforce their own control over people in their neighborhoods and have become accountable to no one. There is no *effective communication* between the people who have different opinions; the only opinion that prevails is the opinion of those with weapons in their hands.

I received a call from José that first night to tell me things were going well and that he would cross the border into Venezuela early in the afternoon on that next day. As simple as that journey sounds, I knew it would be a long journey going from one country to the next. I made that very same journey with him once before. When you approach the bridge that separates the two countries, you must do it on foot. No vehicles of any kind are allowed to drive past a certain point. The expression on the faces of the people whom you see standing in the extremely long lines, leaving or attempting to leave Venezuela, is heartbreaking. It is the vivid expression of the oppression under which Venezuelans live. That border crossing is a land where it's *every-man-for-himself;* where *cooperation* seems to have no foothold at all.

Throughout the next day, I anxiously waited to get a call from José's satellite phone. It was evening and I still had no news. I became more and more concerned with each minute that passed. Time seems to move so slow when we want it to go fast and so fast when we want it to slow down. Later that night, I feared bad news. It was near midnight when I heard my phone ring and saw his satellite phone's ID on the display. I quickly answered it and was so thankful to hear his voice. José explained that he had just crossed the border. I immediately questioned him, "Just now? Why so late?"

He said, "It's a long story; I'll give you some details now and the rest later 'cause I still have to make my way into the country. The bottom line is that I got to the border as soon as I could. I knew I was in trouble when I finally got to the place on the Colombian side where I needed to stamp my passport. The immigration officer told me it was too late to cross into Venezuela. I asked him to stamp my exit anyway and I'd try to figure out a way to cross the border."

I forcefully asked, "Why didn't you stay in Colombia another night?"

José said, "There are no good hotel options around here. I'd have to find my way back into the city and it's too late in the night. Besides, I already arranged for Johnny [his nephew] to meet me on the other side. I had to walk in the dark of night. I ran into a couple of Venezuelan soldiers who didn't seem happy to be there.

They made a point to show me their weapons by pointing their guns at me. They rudely told me to get back to Colombia. I kept on asking them to let me cross the barricades but one of them told me to get lost.

"I kept on going back and forth with them. Soon, a couple of other people wanting to cross the border came up behind me in the dark. One was a lady with a baby in her arms. This whole border scene was sad and stressful. I really felt bad for the lady and the baby being there at that time of the night. I was staring at the soldiers after I ran out of things to say to them. One of the soldiers, who appeared to be in charge, told me to read a sign that said, 'No crossing after 8 PM.' I prayed in my mind for God to help me and the others. It got intense.

"I really was out of things to say to those guys. Then, something just came out of my mouth, 'Hey man, in the spirit of this Holy Week, just let us cross to see our families.' I knew the armed soldier was not happy with any of us who were standing there.

"He looked at me and said, 'If I let you cross, you will just stroll down this bridge and my commandant will get upset with me for letting you cross. Others will see you cross and will come to harass me to let them go cross as you did.'

"I told him, 'Don't worry, man. The commandant won't see us. We'll make sure of that. And nobody else is going to come to you at this late hour.' He laughed sarcastically.

"Then he waved to the other soldier and said to us, 'Ok, cross but I want you running across the bridge. I want you to get lost and I'm not responsible for what happens if you run into other soldiers. Get out of here.'

"We didn't wait. We crossed and ran full speed ahead into complete darkness. Thank God I got to where I am now. But now I have a new problem though, the immigration office is closed and I'm now in the country illegally. I definitely don't want to sleep on the sidewalk tonight and wait until they open the immigration office tomorrow morning. I'm going to my mom's house illegally. I'll deal with that problem tomorrow. I better get going. I'll call again when I can. I love you."

I was so glad that he had called me, but I did not feel much better after he hung up. Knowing he was there was bad enough. Knowing he was there illegally was even worse. I also thought of his mom and dad living there and having to suffer the consequences of other people's actions. The whole ordeal was like having a big heavy cloud over me for several days until José was able to get back.

Several days later, I was so relieved when I finally saw him walk out of the international arrivals terminal at the Atlanta airport. José said he had mixed emotions about being back on U.S. soil. On the one hand, he was sad about his family in Venezuela. On the other, he was glad to be back in a much more stable country.

When people choose to ignore God's universal principles and live outside of the protection that they provide to us, there are serious consequences. Unfortunately, those consequences not only affect the "rule-breakers" but their negative effect often reaches many others. That is why the universal principle of teamwork is so important to each one of us. Societies practice teamwork in order to accomplish common goals while edifying each if its members.

For great teamwork to exist there must be *cooperation* and *effective communication* among the members of the team. When we cooperate with one another, we are choosing to work together to accomplish a common goal. If we nurture this idea of working together, we can multiply our effectiveness in whatever line of work we are in. This is true for a small team of people or for an entire nation.

Every time we bring a group of people together, no matter how small of a group, there will be a diversity of ideas, opinions, and beliefs. *Cooperation* is all about dialoguing about those differences and choosing what each member of the group can contribute to achieving the team's goals. *Effective communication* is about listening to understand and speaking to be understood. However, there is a major difference between communication and *effective communication*. Communication is talking to someone or having a mutual conversation. Effective communication, on the other hand, is truly seeking understanding.

When we really listen to someone else and are willing to cooperate, we are really focusing on understanding that person's ideas, opinions, or beliefs. **Sometimes finding common ground is not easy, but we don't have to see eye to eye to walk arm in arm.**

I have had my share of difficult discussions with family members, coworkers, church members, or neighbors but in the end, I had the option to agree on a course of action. Sometimes, it may have taken a long time to find common ground and a good course of action that was acceptable to everyone involved. When it works out that way, I remind myself that we have the option to agree to disagree until we find the best solution to the issue.

Teamwork is a part of life and we ought to practice being the best team members that we can be within our own circle of friends and beyond. But we must keep in mind that even *the best* or *most* gifted teams will have conflict from time to time. Conflict is neither good nor bad—it is neutral. We must come to grips with the fact that conflict is a common part of life. When conflict surfaces within your group, add some levity to the situation by saying, "let's agree to disagree agreeably." You may get some strange looks, but it may be what the group needs to relax a bit.

I encourage you to look within yourself and find out if you know how to disagree agreeably. If you do, you can teach others, who are less experienced at this than you are. If you do not, you should consider seeking a coach or counselor who can help you develop some skills to deal with conflict. It is likely that the first step will be admitting that you need help in this area. We all have to learn it sooner or later if we want to be effective when working with others.

As climbing companions of Jesus, we are all a work-in-progress and learning to manage conflict move us further down the road of maturity.

We heard about conflict management at school since we were young. But how do we know if we are ready to manage conflict within our own circle of influence? Ask yourself these questions to see where you fall on the conflict-management scale:

- Do I walk away or hide from conflict?
- Do I get angry with others when there is a conflict?
- Do I get sarcastic with others when I conflict with them?
- Do I resent people for creating conflict in my life?

If you answered *yes* to one of the questions above, you are making progress and need to concentrate on how to improve in that particular area. If you answered *yes* to more than one question, I encourage you to find someone who can help you figure out the best way to turn those responses around for the positive. This is part of the process of becoming the peacemaker that Jesus asked us to be. We all can become peacemakers and live by the principle of teamwork; it just takes some effort.

Most conflicts, divorces, wars, broken relationships, etc. are ultimately the result of poor communication and serious mis-understandings. What a person means to say and what others hear can often be two different things. I am speaking of people with good intentions. Dealing with *malicious people* is a whole different topic which I am not addressing here.

Something I picked up along the way that has served me well in life is a simple question that I often ask at meetings or one-on-one conversations. I usually wait until I think I understand what is being said and then I ask, "What I hear you saying is *such and such,* is that correct?" The *such and such* is my best attempt at repeating what I heard the other person say. Sometimes the other party may say, "Exactly, that is what I meant" or sometimes that person may say, "I think you may have misunderstood me." Either way, we both win by having that exchange.

Another variation of the same question is, "Let me reiterate what I hear both of us saying. We are saying *such and such.* Do you agree?" Once again, the other party will either validate that we are on the same track or not. This cycle can be repeated as many times as necessary until we all hear the same thing. At work, I often find myself sending email messages to people with whom I have previously spoken to restate what we said so that we both can see, in writing, those things that we agreed upon. This action takes more time up front but can save a lot of time and heartache later.

Another important step in our quest to become peacemakers is looking deep within ourselves and getting to know our weaknesses and strengths. Our weaknesses are more elusive and harder to find. They can be blind spots in our lives which can become a huge obstacle in our path to becoming peacemakers.

More often than not, it will require help from someone in order to identify our weaknesses. Trusted friends who can be honest with us can be of great help during this process. It is much better if our friends are honest but gentle with their feedback. If our friends do not fit that profile, it is best to book a couple of sessions with a good counselor to fully discover our blind spots. Please trust me when I say that it will be a great investment in yourself.

Our strengths are typically easier to find than our weaknesses, but we need to be just as intentional to clearly identify them. Knowing our strengths helps us become better peacemakers. There are tools online that can help you identify your strengths with a fair amount of accuracy. Your friends can also be of great help as you set out to identify your strengths. Once you are confident that you know your strengths, ask yourself how you can use them to help your team achieve its goals.

Equipped with the knowledge of your strengths and weaknesses, you can become a great team member. You will find yourself striving to cooperate and communicate effectively. You will find more satisfaction as you work with others and others will find great satisfaction in working with you. You will be a bonafide peacemaker.

The Master expects us to be peacemakers so we can fully pursue our God-given purpose in life. We are agents of reconciliation in every situation in which we find ourselves. Those situations can happen in our homes, schools, churches, government buildings, or anywhere we go. We are members of God's family and we represent him. We have been blessed with the coveted title of "Child of God."[6]

The book of Hebrews in the Newer Testament of the Christian scriptures is a letter written by an unknown author to presumably Jewish Italians who were at risk of abandoning their faith because of hardship, persecution, and social pressure. I find it of special interest that the author was concerned about his readers not being people of peace in the face of persecution.

We don't need to travel all the way to Italy (although we would like to) to understand what the writer meant. We can see the same happening in our culture today. When those climbing companions in our own circles of influence are harshly confronted because of their Christian faith, some may respond with harsh words, rude behavior, or even anger. Yet, others may decide that social pressures are too much for them and begin to fall away from their faith.

The writer of Hebrews was responding to news about similar behavior in that part of the world. He instructed and shared a warning with them in two short sentences. I think that instruction and warning apply to us today in the very same way. "Make every effort to live in peace with everyone and to be holy; without holiness no one will see the Lord."[7] It's a big challenge but one that we, climbing companions, ought to conquer.

Jesus was also very clear about expecting his followers to be agents of reconciliation and peace. He told his climbing companions, "You have heard that it was said, 'Love your neighbor and hate your enemy.' But I tell you, love your enemies and pray for those who persecute you, that you may be children of your Father in heaven."[8] Yikes! That stings. We are mandated to love those who are hard to love. We cannot do anything other than loving them because that is what peacemakers do.

The universal principle of teamwork requires that we become the best peacemakers we can ever be. Can you imagine a community or society where the medical world would refuse to cooperate with the business world? Or the educational system would refuse to work with law enforcement? Or the faith-based community would refuse to work with elected officials? It would be anarchy. That is the reason why climbing companions must be peacemakers; our world needs us to be. **When all the different people groupings within a society work together in harmony, it creates a positive and safe environment for everyone.**

Whether we are dealing with a whole nation, like Venezuela, or a single family, the universal principle of teamwork applies in the same way. Sadly, for many children, the greatest place of conflict is their home. Just like a government can create negative consequences for its people, a home can also create an environment with negative consequences for the family. Children are the victims in most cases. Homes, where the adults choose to ignore the principle of teamwork or any other universal principle for that matter, can create anxiety disorders, unhealthy behaviors, bad grades, poor sleeping habits, and more.

When a home is orderly, loving, and peaceful, we don't observe those characteristics in most children. Even when children live in homes without peace, providing a safe haven for children can make a big difference in their lives. Public school classrooms with caring teachers and mentors can bring about stability to a child who may otherwise be lost in a world of fear.

Mentors who take time out of their busy lives and go into public high, middle, or elementary schools to meet with kids and speak truth to them can bring healing to many hurting kids. **We can be agents of reconciliation in our communities, but we must show up to do it.** I am so thankful for the many mentors who partner with us at our non-profit to be equipped so they can show up and work with kids in the schools week after week. The faces of some of the kids whom we mentor are expressionless at times, but their hearts are feeling the love and understanding that caring mentors bring to them.

The world can be a great place if we live as peacemakers each day of our lives. Climbing companions of Jesus must lead the way. Have you ever thought what our Christian community would look like if our pastors would regularly exchange pulpits with other pastors and encourage their church leaders to collaborate with other churches in their community? What a great example that would be to the communities in which we live. The world would see the body of Christ working together and taking full advantage of their talents and gifts just like the apostle Paul encouraged the people of Corinth to do.[9] That is the way of the Master.

* * *

TAKE AWAY: For great teamwork to exist there has to be cooperation and effective communication among the members of the team.

GIVE AWAY: You don't have to see eye to eye to walk arm in arm.

12

Enthusiasm

"Be happy about it! Be very glad! For a great reward awaits you in heaven."[1]

It had been a good night of sleep and I woke up early the next morning ready to take on whatever challenges the day would bring. My traveling companions were eager to get going and were already waiting for me at the hotel breakfast bar by the time I got there. We ate breakfast while discussing the plans for the day.

The team had already filled up our vehicle with gas and other supplies. They nicely but forcefully kept on trying to get me to leave the hotel and quit wasting time. I did not feel that I was wasting time and kept thinking that they needed to chill out. Soon enough, we all walked out of the hotel. They all got in the van and smiled at me as I clipped-in one of the pedals and pushed forward on my bicycle.

I had been riding my bicycle for a couple of weeks and this was another day of that journey (that I previously mentioned in Chapter 2 - Choices and Habits). As I picked up some speed heading east on that small town's main street, it felt different than usual. I was trying to figure out if it was just my imagination or was I more sluggish than usual.

I made a mental note to ask my support team about my speed when I would meet up with them again at one of our designated stops along the route. I was riding through the beautiful State of Wyoming on my way to Georgia and I surely did not want to start losing time. I was to cycle 3,284 miles from the Pacific to the Atlantic Coast and I could not afford to fall behind on my schedule.

The fact that my friends were pushing me to leave as early as possible from the hotel that morning started to worry me as I pedaled. I felt slower than usual. Mornings so far had been cool and invigorating during my trip but not that day. The heat felt hotter and the headwind felt stronger than what I had experienced up to that day.

When you travel west to east across the continental U.S., you expect to have a tailwind for most of your trip; that was not happening to me though. I kept on thinking that it was all my imagination and that I was just worried about how many more miles I still had to pedal before my final destination.

I soon lost sight of the beautiful mountains that surrounded me and my mind zeroed in on the hot pavement in front of me and the pestering headwind that buffeted my face. I pedaled and pedaled but the bike seemed to barely move forward. I asked myself, "What in the world is going on?" I drank as much water as I could push down my throat and kept on pedaling.

Soon, I could hear myself hyperventilating and thoughts of stopping and throwing the bike off to the side of the road crossed my mind. My rational thinking gave up and my thoughts went all over the place, "Who am I kidding? An average middle age woman like me cannot cycle from coast to coast. Nobody cares about why I am doing this ride. This is dumb." My breathing turned to uncontrollable sobbing and I was ready to call it quits.

A quiet voice within me whispered something though. At first, I did not want to pay attention to it, but I knew it would be better if I did. The voice became stronger and suddenly my mind flashed back to a time in my high school years when a friend told me that I was the most negative person she had ever known. Those words really hurt but it was back in those teenage years of my life when I made the decision that I would become a positive person no matter what.

Well, there I was in the middle of beautiful Wyoming riding a bicycle and being negative about my situation and myself. Yes, it was extremely hot. Yes, I had a 20 to 30 mile-per-hour headwind fighting against me. Yes, my legs were hurting. Yes, I had more than 2,000 miles still to ride.

I fought to get my thoughts back in order and let rational thinking prevail once again. I forced myself to think about the principle of enthusiasm. People who live by that principle understand that it takes both *positive thinking* and *proper perspective* to navigate difficult situations. On that bicycle, I knew that I needed to activate those two thought processes in my mind, and I needed to do it quickly.

I started guiding my thoughts through a checklist of positive things that I had such as the support team that was waiting for me up ahead, the latest and greatest type of bicycle that had been partially donated for my trip, the healthy body with which I woke up that morning, the support prayers of my family and friends, and the money that had already been donated to us for troubled kids.

Positive thinking is an amazing thing. One moment you may feel

129

as if you have nothing going for you but then you start feeling your spirit being lifted by all the good things that you are bringing back up to the forefront of your mind.

As the day got hotter and hotter, I guided my mind to remember the reason why I had even organized the trip. I remembered that I had spoken with educators in the public schools and juvenile court administrators and found out that there were thousands of kids on waiting lists waiting for mentors. When I learned that, I realized that I needed to help get mentors for those kids.

Those thoughts also helped me gain the perspective that I needed at that moment. That trip was about those kids and not about me getting some kind of recognition or award. I had prayed about the trip and I had felt 100% confirmed that I needed to do the trip. Having a *proper perspective* is like driving through a foggy segment of a highway and finally getting to the other side; it just brings everything back into clear focus.

The principle of enthusiasm is our best weapon to use against the challenges that can discourage us and bring us down. When we live by this principle, we are not guaranteed to be free from tough or evil things but we will have what it takes to overcome them.

On my cycling trip across America, I later found out that many of my encouragers and supporters were very worried about the weather conditions that our country was experiencing that summer. Some in my support team in Atlanta had been wondering how to go about ending our mission. Forest fires had pushed my route further into Wyoming and added additional miles to my journey instead of my original shorter route across Colorado.

That month of July went on record as the all-time hottest month for the nation in the recorded period that dated back to 1895.[2] As I was cycling, I saw how the extreme dryness and above-average temperatures devastated crops and livestock from the Great Plains to the Midwest.[3]

Challenges will always come our way. Whether it is extreme heat on a 3,200-mile bicycle trip, a discussion with a banker about a denied loan to start our new business, or marriage-related difficulties, we all face challenges on a regular basis. How we face those challenges, and our response to the people involved, is where the principle of enthusiasm comes into play. But enthusiasm does not happen automatically. It is a universal principle that is developed through discipline and over time. It is a consciously adopted way of thinking and living.

It is also worth mentioning that enthusiasm is not a feeling or a personality trait that some people have, and others don't. Instead, it is a well-trained and developed attitude. If it were a feeling, it would not last. The principle of enthusiasm does not depend on feelings, people or circumstances but on the power given to us by the Master. Climbing companions of Jesus work hard at developing lives that have the principle of enthusiasm at their core.

When Jesus Christ taught his climbing companions how they ought to live their lives, he first encouraged them to live by several character traits that many know as the Beatitudes. Then, he distinctly addressed the issue of opposition and persecution. He told them that others were going to insult them, persecute them, lie about them, and say all kinds of evil things about them for no other reason than they were his followers.[4]

I imagine that those early climbing companions were probably shocked to hear those words. After all, it would be natural to think that when you do what God tells you to do, you would have an easier life and people would like you. But Jesus was telling them (and us) that it wasn't so!

Even today, it is sobering to hear how the Master warned us. At the same time, he has commanded us to be joyful and glad amid harsh circumstances. He also revealed to all of us that we will be in good company when that time of persecution comes. He said, "Rejoice and be glad because you have a great reward in heaven! The prophets who lived before you were persecuted in these ways."[5]

That is a completely different way of looking at the ups and downs of life (especially the downs). Jesus commands us to rejoice and be glad regardless of what others do to us. He wants his climbing companions to understand that that is how we ought to behave and expects us to be different than those who are of the world. This way of responding amid challenges is the way of the Master.

You may be thinking, yes, I can work at being positive but pretending to be happy when things are going bad all around me would mean that I must be *fake*. I agree with you 100% on that! We *never* want to be fake. You have probably met people who told you they are realists and do not like playing games with reality. To them (and to you), I want to ask you to look at the difference between enthusiasm and happiness.

Happiness depends on people saying the right things to us, circumstances going our way, and having uplifting feelings. Pretending to be happy in front of others when things are going severely bad is certainly being fake. However, enthusiasm is having joy in our lives based on the teachings and example of Jesus Christ. That joy comes from knowing deep within us "that God causes all things to work together for good to those who love God, to those who are called according to His purpose."[6] With that assurance, you and I know that if we love God, we can then have enthusiastic joy even when we face insurmountable odds. Challenges are still there; happiness may not be present, but enthusiasm and joy can still prevail within us.

To be a person of enthusiasm, we need to train ourselves to think differently. Remember, that it is a choice. A person can be an introvert and still be filled with enthusiasm just as much as a person can be an extrovert and be off-the-charts enthusiastic. We all have the ability to live lives filled with enthusiasm.

My mother taught us, kids, a practice that has stuck with me all my life. It is a good practice that helps us be positive thinkers. I recommend it to anyone who may have a hard time training herself or himself to be filled with enthusiasm. Mom called this practice the giving of *verbal flowers*.

José likes it when we give them as long as I don't call them by those names. He cannot get it through his head that the name is part of the fun. He says that a better name for it would be, *sharing-personal-positive-attributes-about-someone's-character*. Are you kidding me? What kind of name is that?

Regardless of the name, it is the practice of giving sincere words of affirmation to someone else. José and I often organize verbal-flower moments for our staff or friends when we get together to celebrate just about anything. Everyone gets a chance to say something positive about someone else. My mom has always said that it is better to give verbal flowers while someone is alive and can enjoy them instead of waiting to give them at that person's funeral. If you are learning how to be a positive thinker, organize your own verbal-flower moments with those you love. I assure you that everyone will be blessed by the experience.

Another practice that helps us become positive thinkers is to create our own checklist of positive things that we can review when we are confronted by challenging situations. That can work well for us in the spur of the moment. Becoming a positive thinker requires a consistent investment of time and effort but it is well worth the investment. Over time, it becomes a more natural response, but we can only get there after we have made the choice to change our way of thinking. We have to decide that we will train our mind to focus on positive things that result in positive thinking.

There is a positive thinking formula that the apostle Paul shared with climbing companions of Jesus who had become his friends and financial supporters. They lived in the city of Philippi and were facing tough opposition. Paul himself was also facing serious challenges at that time while being detained in Rome right in the center of Caesar's physical domain.

Paul was not speaking from book knowledge or hearsay; he was speaking to his friends from personal experience. He knew what it meant to suffer and yet he had chosen to have enthusiastic joy. Paul's formula or method can be captured in these two sentences: "Fix your thoughts on what is true, and honorable, and right, and pure, and lovely, and admirable. Think about things that are excellent and worthy of praise."[7]

Paul knew that whatever we put into our minds daily will determine what comes out of our mouths during those times of trials and difficulties. We must guard what comes into our minds. Sometimes, we are our own worst enemy when it comes to doing this. We speak out negative things which are not honorable, pure, or admirable. Those very same words come back through our ears and end up finding a nice and secure resting place within our minds.

I encourage you to refuse speaking out negative things. There are positive ways in which we can express ourselves when facing tough and difficult circumstances. Here are some examples:

- That class has so much material to study that it really makes me work hard and learn
- That person has the type of personality that requires that I respond carefully with my words
- This job requires so much of me that I will end up becoming the most diversified employee in the company
- My husband has little patience, but I can see how my patience will get stronger as we both grow together

Those are just a few examples of how we could turn a difficult situation around and see it from a different point of view. Don't take the easy route when it comes to your way of thinking. Frequently, the easy route is not the best route. The easy route, in those examples, would be to say, "I am a realist and I call it as I see it." Saying that is just an excuse so we can be negative and not do the hard work that positive thinking initially requires. Climbing companions of Jesus not only are positive people but they also role model positive thinking when speaking to others.

Children and teens who spend time with us regularly pick up our style of communication and emulate it whether they consciously choose to or not. I urge you to invest in being a person of positive thinking and proper perspective so you can give proper guidance to those younger (and older) than you. Challenge yourself to always be looking for the best thing in every situation and role model that way of thinking to young people around you.

Positive thinking also produces some very tangible benefits that we all can experience. When we become positive thinkers, we start to experience a healthier life with less stress. We feel happier, more peaceful, and grateful. We may even end up living longer because of less stress in our lives. What is not to like about being a positive thinker?

Having a proper perspective is also very important as we become people of enthusiasm. **Proper perspective happens in our lives as we train ourselves to nurture an eternal perspective in all our daily affairs.** In other words, we train our minds to see things from God's point of view. This broadens the dimensions of our circumstances.

Have you ever noticed what happens to a problem once we ask someone else's point of view about it? Frequently, the problem gets easier to solve. Now imagine what can happen when we look at life challenges from God's perspective or point of view. Through that eternal perspective, we can begin to overcome many obstacles.

Early climbing companions were not strangers to suffering and hateful treatment by others. Time and time again we find Christian scriptures and writings about the early days of Christianity that confirm climbing companions' constant exposure to harsh and hateful treatment. Still, time and time again we read about them being joyful. "The apostles left the high council rejoicing that God had counted them worthy to suffer disgrace for the name of Jesus."[8] It was not unusual for early climbing companions to equate persecution with death. Yet, they encouraged each other by looking beyond death and toward eternal.

As we read what Paul wrote to his friends and financial supporters in Philippi, we can see how he slowly but surely had become naturally good at seeing the eternal perspective. He was in chains and rather than complaining about it, he explained how his chains were giving encouragement and boldness to others who were also being persecuted for the cause of Christianity.[9]

Paul probably repeatedly asked himself, "Will this matter in eternity?" If the answer was "yes"; then it would be worthwhile investing time and effort into it. If the answer was "no"; then it did not deserve another minute of his time. We should ask ourselves the same question and, in that way, find the things that merit our time and effort and discard the ones that do not.

If we spend our energy on things we can improve or have control over instead of focusing energy on meaningless things that are out of our control, then our lives can have a more positive impact. By doing this, we become more responsible with our finite resources, become more focused on our significant personal goals, and spend more time following our worthwhile dreams.

I remember a little boy who came to my house one day and told me he was selling special jewels. He showed me some very ordinary little rocks which looked very much like the rocks found in my very own yard. He said they were precious jewels that had come from my yard. I was ready to tell the little boy to go away when another person in my house decided to buy all the rocks and pay 25 cents apiece. I thought to myself, "This does not make sense." As I looked at this little boy and his smile, I quickly realized that this boy was looking at the world as a positive, beautiful, and safe place. Who would I be if I tried to tear that view down for him? I needed to be an energy giver and not an energy taker to that boy who had turned the ordinary into something special.

We must be cautious of the people who intentionally or inadvertently work hard at tearing down our enthusiasm. There are *energy givers* as well as *energy takers* in this world. **Energy givers are positive people who inspire and lead others.** They generally have a smile on their faces and do not mind people being around them.

On the other hand, energy takers are generally negative people.

They primarily only care about themselves and their interests. They tend to exaggerate, gossip, and complain about what others do. They sometimes ask for things that will benefit them but do not want to give when others ask for help.

Climbing companions of Jesus ought to be energy givers who try not to let anything bring them down. They are people of enthusiasm. They brighten everyone's day by their presence and their contributions.

Energy givers understand how to live by the principle of enthusiasm. They take it seriously and renew themselves often. They invest time and effort into their spiritual, mental, emotional, social, and physical renewal so they can have a solid foundation for enthusiasm as they go about doing everything they do.

Living by the principle of enthusiasm requires action. I invite you to take the challenge and strive to be the one who brings positive thinking and a proper perspective to every situation that arises in your home, school, work or social circle. Enthusiasm is essential to Christian life. It is not just good because it benefits us; it is good because it is the way of the Master.

I encourage you to be a person of enthusiasm so you can attract those who do not know the teachings of Jesus Christ. I guarantee you that people will be drawn to you and want to know where your enthusiasm comes from.

By the way, remember that bicycle ride across America? I returned home to an enthusiastic welcome back celebration at one of our high schools. Our city mayor organized an event at the school stadium to thank our team for caring about kids. I cycled my last 20 miles with a police escort and a couple of dozen other cyclists riding with me to celebrate the end of the ride. Local businesses brought gifts to share with people who attended the event. My family came from out of town to celebrate with us. A group of at-risk kids from a home organized a barbeque for the guests. Little kids rode their bicycles on the running track with big smiles on their faces. It was so much fun!

The sensational welcome back celebration reaffirmed for me that the principle of enthusiasm can greatly help us achieve things that, at first, may seem impossible to do. That celebration was filled with so much joy that it made me think about how it will be in heaven when all of us get together for our ultimate and extremely enthusiastic celebration.

* * *

TAKE AWAY: Energy givers are positive people who inspire and lead others.

GIVE AWAY: Bring an eternal perspective to all your daily affairs.

13

Honor

"In that way, you will be acting as true children of your Father in heaven."[1]

"I've become an old man now, and I've preached all over the world. And the older I get, the more I cling to that hope that I started with many years ago."[2]

A t a rare time when all private and commercial aviation over the United States was completely shut down in the aftermath of the 9/11 terrorist attacks, there was only one civilian airplane in the skies. This single civilian aircraft was taking the Reverend Billy Graham to the nation's capital. This single fact gives great credibility to the opinion that says that the late Reverend Billy Graham was the pastor to the whole nation.

Many said that it was a great privilege for Billy Graham to be chosen as the pastor to deliver a message to the nation just three days after the 9/11 attacks. Others have said that the message was a huge responsibility that was placed on his shoulders that day. Yet, others have said that it was a great personal recognition for him to be invited to deliver that message of hope. And, the one thing that most everyone agreed on was that his words brought much-needed comfort to everyone's heart that day.

Rev. Graham's words delivered at the Washington National Cathedral on that September 14 revealed the kind of man he had become. At 80 years old, Billy Graham was not trying to show us how much he had learned and accomplished in his amazing career as a world-renowned speaker. Rather, he was telling every one of us how simple of a life he lived by clinging to the hope given to him by his faith of so many years. He was highlighting neither his achievements nor recognition. Instead, he was encouraging us to be people of faith and hope. Billy Graham speaking to the nation during those very difficult days delivered a great message of blessing and perspective for many of us.

When we meet or learn about people like the Reverend Billy Graham, it does not take much before we think of them as people of honor. To me, honor is a fascinating thing. We read the definition of the word *honor* and quickly grasp its importance. However, reading the definition of the word and making it be a part of our life is not as simple. One could ask, "How do I make honor be a part of our daily life?" or "How did people like Billy Graham become honorable?"

The reason why many of us may struggle with finding a way to make honor a part of our life is because there is no simple 1-2-3 or A-B-C formula that can guarantee us honor from one day to the next.

In the Christian scriptures, we find that the Hebrew word *kabed* is commonly translated as the word honor. A more descriptive translation of that word into English would be the phrase *to give weight*. From that, we can see that the word *kabed* is referring to something great to which we give weight and importance. It is also interesting to know that the scriptures use the same word to describe the glory of God. So, when we talk about a person being honorable, we ought to have very high expectations. Needless to say, no person can ever be compared to God's glory, but we do get the idea that the bar is set very high when we talk about honor.

One thing we know is that honor is what happens to us when we *consistently make the right choices* day after day. An honorable person demonstrates an uncompromising adherence to what is right. Learning about honorable people gives us great insight into how we can strive to be people of honor ourselves.

I developed a lot of interest in the life of Nelson Mandela after a trip to South Africa. I had the opportunity to visit Robben Island in Cape Town, South Africa a few years after the fall of apartheid in that country. Being able to freely walk inside of what used to be a maximum-security prison for political prisoners and convicted criminals was a surreal experience.

As a former Robben Island inmate gave us a tour of what used to be Nelson Mandela's small cell, I found myself becoming increasingly impressed and inspired by the late South African President's life. Today, he is revered by millions of people as an honorable man. By studying Nelson Mandela's life, I started to understand how he earned such reverence and honor. I don't think it was the result of his fame, oratory skills, or political strategies. I think he became a person worthy of honor as a result of his lifetime *consistent commitment to doing the right thing* to bring freedom and unity to the people of South Africa.

Another person for whom I have great admiration is President Abraham Lincoln. I love getting my hands on any biography about President Lincoln. His life was filled with great decisive moments which propelled him to become the 16th President of the United States of America. His life inspires me and encourages me to stay the course and be a person of integrity regardless of the circumstances. Before and after becoming president, Abraham Lincoln gave high priority to maintaining his integrity, above all else. His *consistency in making the right choices* since his younger years earned him the nickname *Honest Abe*. During his presidential campaign, his supporters even used that nickname as his campaign slogan. I always think of President Lincoln as a person of honor because of his steadfastness to doing the right thing in the face of much controversy and opposition.

I read about Queen Isabella I of Castille (modern-day Spain) and became interested in her life and her accomplishments. There is no way for me to know whether Queen Isabella was concerned about her reputation back in the mid to late 1400s. But I do know that Queen Isabella led the creation of a powerful and unified state of Spain with influence that spread to the newly discovered Americas. Her influence greatly determined the missionary journeys by many priests who came to the American continent with the express purpose of sharing and teaching the gospel of Jesus Christ to foreigners.

Isabella's determination to bring order to a nation in chaos and her strong commitment to serving her Christian faith through her royal decisions made her legacy live for centuries after her death. Her reputation truly lived in many places at one time and it even transcended many cultures throughout Europe, the Americas, and other places around the world. The result of her consistent choices and commitment to her faith made her a person worthy of honor across many different cultures. Queen Isabella's reputation makes me think that she strived to act as an active citizen of the kingdom of God and one of God's children.

A word that comes up when talking about honor is the word *reputation* which you may have also heard referred to as *having a good name.*

The book of Proverbs tells us about the value of a good name, "A good name is more desirable than great riches; to be esteemed is better than silver or gold.[3] Our choices determine our reputation. My good friend and ministry partner, Felisha, once gave a talk to a group of young ladies on the value of our reputation. She spoke of a concept that I think every young person needs to learn and fully comprehend. The concept describes our reputation as the thing that has the ability to be in two or more places at any single moment in time. You may ask, "How can that be?" The answer is profound yet simple.

The choices we make as we live our daily lives create our reputation. Those who come in contact with us can quickly see the result of our choices, decisions, and actions. It is at each of those encounters with other people that they begin drafting a picture in their minds of what our reputation looks like. That picture stays there long after we have left their presence. Once we come in contact with others, the same process repeats itself and our picture once again remains with them after we leave.

Our reputation, that picture of us in people's minds, will continue to live in some capacity or another regardless of whether we are physically there or not. At any given time, our reputation may be discussed by others in two or more different places whether we know it or not. I believe it should be our priority to live our lives in such a way that our reputation is built on what is right and pleasing to God. Those who build a life reputation by consistently making the right choices based on truth will sooner or later become people worthy of honor.

Have you asked yourself lately what kind of reputation you

have been building with your life choices? I make an effort to ask myself that question every so often. I also look for people in whom I can trust and give them permission to speak honestly about what they see in me and my life. Asking others, who are known for having wisdom and discernment, to give us truthful feedback about our reputation is a great way for us to sharpen our behavior and improve our reputation.

As the Lord Jesus Christ was walking in the flesh on this earth, he gave his climbing companions, those who were following him on that mountain so long ago, a list of behaviors that are to be lived out by those who want to be called God's children. He told them, "In that way, you will be acting as true children of your Father in heaven."[4]

Then, the Master also challenged them to make it a goal to be single-minded as genuine citizens of the kingdom of God. He called us to be perfect just as our Father in heaven is perfect.[5] That concept of perfection is better understood by us when we think of it as godlikeness or the act of living a godly life.

Living a godly life is the application to our lives of the universal principles that Jesus expects all his followers to apply with equal fervor and commitment. Those universal truths were applicable back then, when he first shared them, just as they are applicable now for, they are true for anyone, anywhere and anytime.

When you take time to think about the future, what picture do you have of your future self? That picture that you have in your mind that can act as a *north star* in your life Get that north star picture clear in your mind and write it down in your journal and/or favorite electronic device so you can review it often. Pray daily over it.

If you have never done this before, start with a couple of simple phrases or statements that describe what you want your life to look like 5, 10, or 20 years from now. When we consistently make wise choices, we will begin, little by little, seeing that picture become a reality in our lives.

I hope that by reading this book you have been encouraged to grow as a climbing companion of Jesus. Climbing companions are representatives of God and His Kingdom on this earth. Therefore, our north star picture should reflect godly qualities such as respect, integrity, self-control, courage, humility, excellence, compassion, enthusiasm, teamwork, and culminate with honor. A person of honor is not a person who lives life accidentally.

Dare not to conform to the patterns of this world as you continue to walk in the way of the Master.

* * *

TAKE AWAY: Get a picture in your mind that acts as your north star and follow it daily.

GIVE AWAY: Invite others to walk in the way of the Master.

Notes

The Invitation

1. Isaiah 55:11 (NLT)
2. Deuteronomy 6:6-9
3. Isaiah 55:11 (NIV)
4. Isaiah 55:8-9 (NIV)
5. Deuteronomy 6:1
6. Matthew 5:1-2 (TM)

Universal Principles

1. Matthew 5:1-2 (TM)
2. Matthew 5:1-2 (TM)
3. Matthew 5:13-16
4. Deuteronomy 6:6-9 (TM)
5. John 4:38
6. Ephesians 6:10-18
7. Matthew 5:3-4
8. Psalm 34:19 (NIV)
9. Luke 12:48 (ASV)

Choices and Habits

1. Romans 12:1-2 (TM)
2. Matthew 5:8
3. Darren Hardy, *Compound Effect* (Lake Dallas: Success Books, 2010), p. 23.
4. Will Durant, *The Story of Philosophy: The Lives and Opinions of the World's Greatest Philosophers,* (Pocket Books, 2nd ed., 1991)
5. Maltz, Maxwell, *Psycho-Cybernetics.* Narrated by Matt Furey, https://www.youtube.com/watch?v=c0kUrbx2JaQ, 2017. Audiobook.
6. Phillippa Lally and colleagues, Research Department of Behavioural Science and Health, University College London, UK. Phillippa Lally is a health psychology researcher at University College London. In a study published in the European Journal of Social Psychology, Lally and her research team performed an experiment in order to determine how long it takes to form a habit.
7. Stephen Covey, *The 7 Habits of Highly Effective People,* (Free Press, 2004)
8. Lori Salierno, *Hope Dangerously* (Celebrate Life International, Inc., 2012)
9. Marjorie J. Thompson, *Soul Feast: An Invitation to the Christian Spiritual Life,* (Louisville: Westminster John Knox Press, 1995) p. xix

Respect

1. Matthew 7:12 (NIV)
2. 1 Peter 2:13-17
3. Matthew 7:12 (NIV)
4. Ephesians 4:2-3
5. Aretha Franklin's website: https://www.arethafranklin.net/

Integrity

1. Matthew 5:8 (TM)
2. Edgar Allan Poe, *The Tell-Tale Heart*, (1843)
3. Matthew 6:1
4. Matthew 7:24
5. Ephesians 2:15-16 (NIV)
6. Ephesians 5:8-9
7. Ephesians 5:13
8. James M. Kouzes, Barry Z. Posner, *Credibility: How Leaders Gain and Lose it, Why People Demand it* (San Francisco: Jossey Bass, 1993), p. 14
9. Genesis 39
10. Genesis 39:9 (NIV)
11. Genesis 39
12. 2 Samuel 11
13. 2 Samuel 22
14. Luke 22:31-33
15. Matthew 26:34 (NLT)
16. Matthew 16:18

Self-Control

1. Matthew 5:5 (NASB)
2. Matthew 5:5 (NASB)
3. 1 Corinthians 10:13

Courage

1. Matthew 5:10 (NIV)
2. Translated from the word Mosioatunya (Mosi-Oa-Tunya), the Makololo name for Victoria Falls on what is now the border between Zambia and Zimbabwe.
3. Isaiah 48:13 (NLT)
4. Daniel 6:21-23
5. Daniel 3:28
6. Joshua 2
7. Exodus 1:15-21
8. Matthew 5:10 (NRSV)
9. Hebrews 13:5-6 (TM)
10. Jeremiah 29:11
11. 1 Samuel 17:46 (NIV)
12. Philippians 1:21 (NLT)
13. Philippians 4:8
14. *No Peaceful Warriors!* by Ambrose Redmoon (1991)

Excellence

1. Matthew 5:6 (NASB)
2. Matthew 5:6 (NASB)
3. Luke 18:1-8
4. Centers for Disease Control and Prevention (CDC) https://www.cdc.gov/mmwr/volumes/67/wr/mm6722a1.htm
5. Sam Parker, *212: The Extra Degree* (The Walk the Talk Company, 2011)
6. Charles Paul Conn, Making it Happen (F.H. Revell Co, 1981)

Compassion

1. Matthew 5:7 (NIV)
2. Matthew 5:7 (NIV)
3. Matthew 25:35-40
4. Leviticus 25:8-13
5. A noun. South Africa English. An older female authority figure
6. James 5:11
7. James 1:19–27; 2:14–26
8. Mary T. Lathrap, Judge Softly (1895)

Humility

1. Matthew 5:3-4 (TM)
2. 1 Peter 5:6 (NLT)
3. Romans 12:1 (NIV)
4. 1 John 2:16 (ESV)

5. John 13:5
6. Matthew 5:3-4 (NIV)
7. Romans 12:3
8. Psalm 139:13-16 (NIV)
9. John 3:30 (NIV)
10. John 3:27 (NLT)
11. Unpublished paper by professor Bruce Ware, Fuller Theological Seminary.
12. Ephesians 2:10 (NIV)

Teamwork

1. Matthew 5:9 (TM)
2. U.S. Department of State – Bureau of Consular Affairs' website https://travel.state.gov/content/travel/en/traveladvisories/tra travel-advisory.html
3. The Bible does not reveal the exact location of the Sermon on the Mount. It has been historically believed to have been on Mount Eremos which is located on the northwestern shore of the Sea of Galilee, between Capernaum and Gennesaret (Ginosar), on the southern slopes of the Korazim Plateau. This location is often called the Mount of Beatitudes.
4. Matthew 5:9 (TM)
5. Venezuelan Violence Observatory (Observatorio Venezolano de Violencia – OVV)
6. Matthew 5:9 (NRSV)
7. Hebrews 12:14 (NIV)
8. Matthew 5:43-45 (NIV)
9. 1 Corinthians 12

Enthusiasm

1. Matthew 5:12 (NLT)
2. NOAA National Centers for Environmental Information, State of the Climate: National Climate Report for July 2012, published online August 2012, retrieved from https://www.ncdc.noaa.gov/sotc/national/201207.
3. NOAA National Centers for Environmental Information, State of the Climate: National Climate Report for July 2012, published online August 2012, retrieved from https://www.ncdc.noaa.gov/sotc/national/201207.
4. Matthew 5:11
5. Matthew 5:12
6. Romans 8:28 (NASB)
7. Philippians 4:8 (NLT)
8. Acts 5:41 (NLT)
9. Philippians 1:12-14

Honor

1. Matthew 5:45 (NLT)
2. Words spoken by the Reverend Billy Graham's during his 9/11 Message from the Washington National Cathedral on September 14, 2001. https://billygraham.org/story/a-day-to-remember-a-day-of-victory/
3. Proverbs 22:1
4. Matthew 5:45 (NLT)
5. Matthew 5:48 (NIV)